SOMERSET

A GENEALOGICAL BIBLIOGRAPHY

— BY —

STUART RAYMOND

FEDERATION OF FAMILY HISTORY SOCIETIES

Published by the
Federation of Family History Societies,
c/o The Benson Room, Birmingham and Midland Institute,
Margaret Street, Birmingham B3 3BS, England.

Copies also obtainable from
S.A. and M.J. Raymond, 6 Russet Avenue, Heavitree, Exeter EX1 3QB, U.K.
S.A. and M.J. Raymond, P.O. Box 255, Belmont, Vic. 3216, Australia.

Printed by Parchment (Oxford) Limited.

Cataloguing in publication data:

Raymond, Stuart A., 1945-
Somerset: a genealogical bibliography.
British genealogical bibliographies.
Birmingham, England: Federation of Family History Societies, 1991.

DDC 016.9291094238

ISBN 1 872094 22 8

ISSN: 1033-2065

CONTENTS

INTRODUCTION

This bibliography is intended primarily for genealogists. It is, however, hoped that it will also prove useful to local historians, librarians, research students, and anyone else interested in the history of Somerset and Somersetians. It is designed to be used in conjunction with my English genealogy: an introductory bibliography, which lists general works relating to the whole country, and with the other volumes in the British genealogical bibliographies series.

Many genealogists, when they begin thier research, do not realise just how much material is available in print. And they not infrequently head first for the archives, whereas they would probably do better to consult printed works first. When faced with the vast array of tomes held by libraries such as that of the Somerset Archaeological and Natural History Society, it is difficult to know where to begin. This bibliography, in conjunction with others in the series, is designed to assist in finding that beginning, and to provide guidance in following through the quest for ancestors. In general, I have not included works which are national in scope, but which have Somerset content. Such works may be identified in my English genealogy: an introductory bibliography. I have also excluded the innumerable notes and queries found in such journals as G.T. and N.Q.S.D., except where the content is of importance. Where I have included such notes, replies to them are cited in the form 'see also', with no reference to the names of respondents. Local and church histories have also been excluded, except in a few cases. Such histories are frequently invaluable for genealogical purposes, but a full listing would require another volume.

Be warned - I cannot claim that this bibliography is comprehensive. Some things I have deliberately excluded; others I have undoubtedly missed. If you come across anything which should be included, please let me know.

Most of the works listed here are readily available in the libraries listed below - although no library holds everything. Even if you are overseas, you should be able to find copies of the more important works in larger research libraries. However, some items may prove difficult to locate - particularly articles in local periodicals. Never fear! Do not despair of discovering the whereabouts of relevant published information. Genealogists should expect, indeed, insist, that their local library participate in the international inter-library loan system. Librarians believe, as an article of faith, that all published material should be universally available; your local library should be able to obtain most of the items listed here, even if it has to go overseas to get them.

The work of compiling this bibliography has depended heavily on the resources of the libraries I have used. These included the Somerset County Library's local collection, and the

Somerset Archaeological & Natural History Society's library,
both at Taunton Castle, the West Country Studies Library, the
Devon & Exeter Institution, Bristol Reference Library, Exeter
University Library, and Bristol University Library. The idea
for this book took shape whilst I was employed at Deakin
University Library, in Australia, and had the use of the State
Library of Victoria. I am grateful to the librarians of all
these institutions for their help. I am also grateful to Brian
Christmas for proof-reading this book.

Stuart A. Raymond

LIBRARIES AND RECORD OFFICES

The major libraries and record offices concerned with Somersetshire history and genealogy are:

Somerset Archaeological & Natural History Society,
The Castle,
TAUNTON,
Somerset,
TA1 4AD

Somerset County Library,
The Castle,
TAUNTON,
Somerset,
TA1 4AD

Somerset Record Office,
Obridge Road,
TAUNTON,
Somerset,
TA2 7PU

Westcountry Studies Library,
Exeter Central Library,
Castle Street,
EXETER,
Devon, EX4 3PQ.

Devon and Exeter Institution,
7, The Close,
EXETER,
Devon, EX4 4PT.

Most branches of Somerset County Library hold local studies materials.

ABBREVIATIONS

G.T.   <u>Greenwood tree</u>

M.G.H.   <u>Miscellanea genealogica et heraldica</u>

N.Q.S.D.   <u>Notes & queries for Somerset & Dorset</u>

S.A.N.H.   <u>Somerset Archaeology & natural history</u>

S.A.N.H.S   <u>Somersetshire Archaeological and Natural History Society proceedings</u>

CHAPTER 1
THE HISTORY OF SOMERSET

How did your ancestors live, work, eat, and sleep? If you want to know the answer to questions like this, and to understand the world of parish registers, wills, subsidy rolls, and estate surveys, then you need to read up on local history. The good genealogist is always able to place his ancestors in the context of their social setting. For Somerset, a good beginning is provided by:

DUNNING, R. W. A history of Somerset. 2nd ed. Bridgwater: Somerset County Library, 1987.

The same author is responsible for the very detailed parochial histories provided in the Victoria County History:

A history of the county of Somerset. Oxford: Oxford University Press for the Institute of Historical Research, 1974-85. [v.1: Natural history & geology; v.2: Ecclesiastical, political, & socio-economic history, etc; v.3: Kingsbury (east), Pitney, Somerton & Tintinhull hundreds; v.4. Crewkerne, Martock, & South Petherton hundreds; v.5: Whitley (part) & Williton and Freemanors hundreds]

A much older work, which includes a parochial survey and many pedigrees, with extracts from monumental inscriptions, wills. etc, is:

COLLINSON, John. The history and antiquities of the county of Somerset ... Bath: R. Cruttwell, 1791. [Reprinted with new introduction by Robert Dunning, including the index of 1898, and 1939 supplement, Gloucester: Alan Sutton, 1983. For the 1898 index printed separately, see: PEARCE, Edwin. Index to Collinson's history of Somerset, ed. F. W. Weaver & E. H. Bates, including a supplemental index (alphabet and ordinary) to all the armorial bearings mentioned in the work, by J. R. Bramble. Taunton: Barnicott and Pearce, 1898]

See also:

PHELPS, W. The history and antiquities of Somersetshire, being a general and parochial survey of that interesting county. 4 vols. London: J. B. Nichols & Son, 1836-9. [Vols.1 & part of 2 only published]

GERARD, Thomas. The particular description of the county of Somerset, ed. E. H. Bates. Somerset Record Society, 15. Taunton: the Society, 1900.

Valuable scholarly works, providing much useful background information, are provided by:

HAVINDEN, Michael. The Somerset landscape. Making of the English landscape. London: Hodder & Stoughton, 1981.

BETTEY, J. H. Rural life in Wessex, 1500-1900. Bradford on Avon: Moonraker Press, 1977.

HEMBRY, Phyllis May. The Bishops of Bath and Wells, 1540-1640: social and economic problems. London: Athlone Press, 1967.

BARNES, Thomas Garden. Somerset, 1625-1640: a county's government during the 'personal rule'. Cambridge, Mass: Harvard University Press, 1961.

UNDERDOWN, David. Somerset in the civil war and interregnum. Newton Abbot: David & Charles, 1973.

QUAIFE, G. R. Wanton wenches and wayward wives: peasants and illicit sex in early seventeenth century England. London: Croom Helm, 1979.

Two works dealing with particular regions of the county are:

MACDERMOTT, Edward R. T. The history of the Forest of Exmoor. Rev. ed. Newton Abbot: David & Charles, 1973. [Includes list of wardens, etc., and a suitors roll of 1797]

CHADWYCK HEALEY, Charles E. H. The history of the part of West Somerset comprising the parishes of Luccombe, Selworthy, Stoke Pero, Porlock, Culborne, and Oare. London: Henry Sotheran & Co., 1901. [Includes pedigrees, wills, inquisitions post mortem, etc.]

The historical uses of genealogical sources are demonstrated in a number of works:

COLLIS, I. P., & SHORROCKS, D. M., eds. Studies in Somerset history, from local records: the work of members of sessional courses held in the Somerset Record Office ... Bristol: University of Bristol Dept. of Extra-Mural Studies, [1972]. [Contents: PEDEN, Joan D. The apprentices of Pitminster. PEDEN, Joan D. Pitminster: the 1851 census. HAMER, John H. For the defence of the community: the Wiveliscombe Corps of Volunteers, 1803-5. SHERREN, Margaret. Edward and Mary Clarke of Chipley. SLATER, Kathryn. The Catholic Chapel, Taunton, 1822-1878. MUNCKTON, Thelma. Somerset probate inventories, 1729-1747. ALLEN, Margaret. John Bowen of Bridgwater]

JACKSON, S. 'Population change in the Somerset-Wiltshire border area, 1701-1800: a regional demographic study', Southern history, 7, 1985, p.119-44.

JORDAN, W. K. 'The forming of the charitable institutions of the West of England: a study of the changing pattern of social aspirations in Bristol and Somerset, 1480-1660', Transactions of the American Philosophical Society, N.S., 50(8), 1960, p.1-99.

McCALLUM, D. M. 'A demographic study of the parishes of Bruton and Pitcombe', S.A.N.H.S., 121, 1977, p.77-87. [16-19th c.]

SCOTT, R. G. 'Population and enclosure in the mid-nineteenth century: the example of Exmoor', Local population studies, 13, 1974, p.31-40.

Many Somersetians have left their green hills for other lands across the sea. For assistance in tracing them, consult the works listed in chapter 16 of my English genealogy: an introductory bibliography. One work in particular stands out, and is essential for tracing Somersetians down under:

CHUK, F. The Somerset years. Ballarat: Pennard Hill pubs., 1987. [Lists government assisted emigrants from Somerset and Bristol who arrived in Australia 1839-54.]

9

CHAPTER 2
BIBLIOGRAPHY AND ARCHIVES

The standard bibliography for the history of Somerset is:

GREEN, Emanuel. Bibliotheca Somersetensis: a catalogue of books, pamphlets, broadsides in some way connected with the county of Somerset. 3 vols. Taunton: Barnicott & Pearce, 1902. [Contents: Vol. 1. Bath books. Vol.2. County books, Bath excepted, A-K. Vol. 3. County books, Bath excepted, L-Z. General index]

A modern bibliography covering the modern county of Avon, which included a number of historic Somerset parishes, is:

MOORE, J., ed. Avon local history handbook. Chichester: Phillimore, 1979.

A slightly more up-to-date list is provided by:

Somerset books in print. Taunton: Somerset County Library, 1983.

For Bath, see:

A selection of books on Bath. Bath: Bath Municipal Libraries, 1972.

Many historical documents, and especially wills, both published and unpublished, are listed by parish in:

HUMPHREYS, Arthur L. Somersetshire parishes: a handbook of historical references to all places in the county. 2 vols. London: [?], 1906.

An important collection of books and documents is held by the Somerset Archaeological & Natural History Society (the books are still at Taunton Castle, but the documents are now located at the Somerset Record Office). See:

PHIPPS, H. R. 'Documents and deeds in the library at Taunton Castle', S.A.N.H.S., 72(2), 1926, p.68-72. See also: BIDGOOD, William. Index-catalogue of the library of the Somersetshire Archaeological and Natural History Society, Taunton Castle. Taunton: Barnicott, 1889, and PHIPPS, H. R. 'Somerset records', Genealogists magazine, 6, 1932-4, p.90-1.

A useful collection of family histories is held by the Somerset & Dorset Family History Society. See:

GREEN, P. 'Family trees and papers in the library', G.T., 13(3), 1988, p.91. [An up to date print-out of the Society's catalogue is available]

The major repository for Somerset archives is the Somerset Record Office. Its holdings were listed annually in:

'The Somerset Record Office: list of main manuscript accessions ...', S.A.N.H.S., 104-33, 1959-89, passim.

For the office's genealogical holdings, see:

SOMERSET RECORD OFFICE. Primary genealogical holdings in the Somerset Record Office. Taunton: the Office, 1978.

SOMERSET COUNTY COUNCIL. COUNTY RECORDS COMMITTEE. Interim handlist of Somerset quarter sessions documents and other official records preserved in the Somerset Record Office, Shire Hall, Taunton. Taunton: King, 1947.

See also:

HOLMES, T. Scott. A report to the Convocation of the Province of Canterbury on the ecclesiastical records of the Diocese of Bath and Wells, to which is attached a short account of the church plate now in the custody of the Dean and Chapter of Wells and of the parochial clergy of Somerset. Taunton: Barnicott & Pearce, 1914.

JEAFRESON, John Cordy. 'The manuscripts of the county of Somerset in the keeping of the Lord Lieutenant and Custos Rotulorum of the shire', Seventh report of the Royal Commission on Historical manuscripts. C.2340. London: H.M.S.O., 1879, p.692-701. [Also available as a Parliamentary paper]

SHORROCKS, Derek. 'Maritime history research resources in the West Country maritime archives at the Somerset Record Office, Maritime South West, 2, 1986, p.47-50.

The papers of a number of Somerset families are listed in:

RALPH, Elizabeth. Guide to the Bristol Archives Office. Bristol: Bristol Corporation, 1971.

The diocese of Bristol included the parish of Abbotsleigh in Somerset; its records also include papers relating to Diocesan property in Somerset. See:

KIRBY, I. M., ed. Diocese of Bristol: a catalogue of the records of the Bishop and Archdeacons and of the Dean and Chapter. Bristol: Bristol Corporation, 1970.

The contents of an important repository are noted in:

K., S. W. 'Somerset archives at Lambeth Palace Library', N.Q.S.D., 3, 1893, p.217.

Frome Society for Local Study has compiled an index of names from various sources - wills, deeds, directories, tax records, etc - which is described in:

HARVEY, J. H. 'North East Somerset index', Genealogists Magazine, 18(10), 1979, p.353.

CHAPTER 3
JOURNALS AND NEWSPAPERS

Every genealogist with Somerset ancestors should subscribe to:

The Greenwood Tree: newsletter of the Somerset and Dorset Family History Society. Shaftesbury: the Society, 1975–

A small area of the historic county of Somerset is covered by:

Journal of the Bristol and Avon Family History Society. Bristol: the Society, 1975–

Many substantial papers of genealogical relevance, not all of which are listed here, are contained in:

Somersetshire Archaeological and Natural History Society proceedings. Taunton: the Society, 1851–1973. [This is continued by Somerset archaeology and natural history, 1973– , and is indexed in: A short index, chiefly topographical, to the Proceedings of the Somersetshire Archaeological and Natural History Society, vols. I–LXX, to which is added, a parochial index to the inventory of Somerset church plate, published in the Proceedings, 1897–1913. Taunton: Wessex Press, 1937. This is continued by: HALDANE, L. A. General index to volumes 81 to 115 (1935–1971) of the Proceedings of the Somersetshire Archaeological and Natural History Society. Castle Cary: Castle Cary Press, 1972, and 'General index to volumes 116 to 126 (1972–1981)', S.A.N.H.S., 126, 1981–2, p.153–66.]

Many brief notes and queries, together with some more substantial papers, are in:

Notes & queries for Somerset and Dorset. Sherborne: N.Q.S.D., 1890– [This is indexed in: A short index to Somerset and Dorset notes and queries, vols.1–22 (1888–1938). Sherborne: Sawtells for S.D.N.Q., 1942. See also: ELRINGTON, C. R. 'One hundred years of Somerset and Dorset notes and queries', N.Q.S.D., 32, 1986–, p.689–94.]

A useful local journal is:

Bath Natural History and Antiquarian Field Club proceedings. Bath: the Club, 1868–1909. [This is indexed in: JAMIESON, A. W. 'Bath Natural History and Antiquarian Field Club procedings: index to volumes I to IX [1867–1901]', B.N.H.A.F.C. Proceedings., 9, 1901, p.317–23.]

Somerset newspapers are listed in:

BROOKE, L. E. J. Somerset newspapers, 1725–1960. Yeovil: the author, 1960.

CHAPTER 4
PLACE-NAMES AND DIALECT

Where is Cuttlesham? Obscure place-names are constantly cropping up in genealogical study, and need to be identified. There is not, unfortunately, an adequate dictionary of Somerset place-names. A general discussion is, however, provided by:

HILL, James S. The place-names of Somerset. Bristol: St. Stephens Printing Works, 1914.

For the Frome district, see:

McGARVIE, M. Frome place-names: their origins and meaning. Frome: Frome Society for Local Study, 1983.

To identify locations on Exmoor, see:

ALLEN, Noel, & GIDDENS, Caroline. Exmoor locations: an index of Exmoor places. Minehead: Alcombe Books, 1982.

You may also need to discover the meanings of dialect words. A number of glossaries are available:

JENNINGS, J. D. The dialect of the West of England, particularly Somersetshire, with a glossary of words now in use there ... 2nd. ed. London: J. R. Smith, 1869.

WILLIAMS, Wadham Pigott & JONES, William Arthur. A glossary of provincial words and phrases in use in Somersetshire. London: Longmans Green, Reader & Dyer; Taunton: F. May, 1873.

ELWORTHY, Frederick Thomas. The West Somerset word-book: a glossary of dialectal and archaic words and phrases used in the west of Somerset and East Devon. London: English Dialect Society, 1886.

COX, J. Stevens. An Ilchester word list and some folklore notes: a glossary of words, phrases, and rhymes used at Ilchester and recorded before 1925. St. Peter Port: Toucan Press, 1974.

SWEETMAN, George. A glossary of words used by the rural population of Wincanton, Somerset. Wincanton: the author, 1891.

CHAPTER 5
BIOGRAPHICAL DICTIONARIES, AND
OCCUPATIONAL SOURCES, ETC.

Biographical dictionaries provide brief biographical information on the individuals listed. Innumerable such dictionaries exist, and are of considerable value to the genealogist. To identify them, consult my English genealogy: an introductory bibliography. A number of biographical dictionaries are devoted to Somersetians:

Who's who in Somerset. Hereford: Wilson & Phillips, 1934.

GASKELL, Ernest. Somerset leaders, social and political. [   ]: Queenhithe Pub Co., c.1908.

HUMPHREYS, A. L. The Somerset roll: an experimental list of worthies, unworthies, and villains born in the county. London: Strangeways, 1897.

STACEY, Claude. Men of the West: a pictorial who's who of the distinguished, eminent and famous men of the West Country, embracing the counties of Cornwall, Devon, Somerset, Dorset, Wilts and Gloucester, including the city of Bristol. London: Claude Stacey, 1926.

Other useful works include:

ESCOTT, T. H. S. Somerset: historical, descriptive, biographical. Bournemouth: W. Mate & Sons, 1908.

PRESS, C. A. M. Somersetshire lives: social and political. London: Gaskill Jones & Co., 1894.

THURSTON, E. J. The magistrates of England and Wales: western circuit, Cornwall, Devonshire, Dorsetshire, Hampshire, Somersetshire, Wiltshire. Hereford: Jakemans, 1940. [Who's who style of listing]

FISHER, W. G. Somerset worthies, 1: thirty selections. Somerset folk series, 27. London: Folk Press, 1927.

BOGER, Mrs. E. Myths, scenes and worthies of Somerset. London: George Redway, 1887.

BATES HARBIN, E. H. 'Centenarians in Somersetshire', N.Q.S.D., 16, 1920, p.85-8. See also p.147-51.

BATES, E. H. 'Somerset and Dorset gentry', N.Q.S.D., 4, 1894-5, p.355-7 & 5, 1896-7, p.15-17.

DELDERFIELD, W. R. West country historic houses and their families. Newton Abbot: David & Charles, 1970. [v.1: Cornwall, Devon & West Somerset. v.2: Dorset, Wiltshire & North Somerset]

MEEHAN, J. F. Famous houses of Bath and district. Bath: B. & J.F. Meehan, 1901. [This and its supplement, More famous houses of Bath and district (1906), contains much information on gentle families]

If you are searching a particular surname, it may be that another researcher has already collected substantial information. Researchers who have collected information on particular surnames are listed in:

'Family histories', G.T., 13(3), 1988, p.91.

In addition to these general works, there are many publications which provide information relating to various trades and professions. In the early modern period, every trade had its apprentices. These may often be identified in parochial records. For Somerset apprentices who left the parish, and, indeed, the county, see:

'Apprentices from Somerset bound at Carpenters' Hall, London, 1654-1694', N.Q.S.D., 14, 1915, p.98-102.

Calendar of the Bristol apprentice book, 1532-1565. 2 vols. Bristol Record Society, 14 & 33. Bristol: the Society, 1949-1980.

Trade tokens are another source which may be used to identify tradesmen of various sorts. In an age when coinage was not as readily available as it is today, tokens were frequently issued instead. Lists of surviving tokens, which are effectively lists of tradesmen, are provided by a number of articles:

BIDGOOD, William. 'Somerset trade tokens of the seventeenth century, and of the period from 1787 to 1817', S.A.N.H.S., 32(2), 1886, p.115-54. [Reprinted Taunton: T. M. Hawkins, c.1886]

GILL, H. S. 'Seventeenth century Somersetshire tokens', Numismatic chronicle, N.S., 19, 1879, p.99-107.

GRAY, H. St. George. 'Somerset trade tokens, XVI century: new types and varieties, and corrections of former lists', S.A.N.H.S., 61(2), 1915, p.115-27.

SYDENHAM S. 'Bath token issues of the 17th century', Proceedings of the Bath Natural History & Antiquarian Field Club, 10, 1905, p.423-505.

SYDENHAM, S. 'Bath tokens of the 18th century', Spinks numismatic circular, 12, 1904, p.7371-6, 7437-44, & 7511-6. [For the 19th century, see 13, 1905, p.8185-91, 8268-73, & 8395-401. See also 16, 1908, p.10670-72.]

SYMONDS, Henry. 'Taunton tokens of the seventeenth century', S.A.N.H.S., 57(2), 1911, p.54-65.

Tokens were issued by many different trades. For innkeepers, see:

MINNITT, S. C., DURNELL, J., & GUNSTONE, A. J. H. Somerset public house tokens. Bridgwater: Somerset County Council Library Service, 1985.

Winesellers are listed in:

FRY, Geo. S. 'Licences for sale of wine and tobacco ...', N.Q.S.D., 8, 1903, p.88-90. [In Somerset and Dorset, 1625-35]

The advent of tobacco meant a demand for clay pipes. Pipe-makers are listed in a number of works:

OWEN, M. B. 'Clay tobacco pipes from Bath', S.A.N.H.S., 111, 1966-7, p.51-5. [Includes brief list of pipe makers]

BROWN, P. S., & Dorothy N. 'Tobacco-pipe makers of Bath in the 19th century', N.Q.S.D., 30, 1974-9, p.24-30. [Includes names from directories, poll books, & census returns; supplemented by: BROWN, P. S. & SNEDDON, J. M. 'Clay tobacco pipes from Bath', N.Q.S.D., 30, 1974-9, p.165-9.]

Millers are identified in two works:

COULTHARD, Alfred J., & WATTS, Martin. Windmills of Somerset and the men who worked them. London: Research Publishing, 1978. [Includes index of millers and men, with pedigrees of Spearing, Stevens-Loader, & Wilkins]

ROGERS, K. H. Wiltshire and Somerset woollen mills. Edington: Pasold Research Fund, 1976. [Includes gazetteer, with brief histories of mills, giving names of many millers]

The names of mariners in Bristol and Somerset, 1570, are given in:

DAMER POWELL, J. W. 'Somerset ships', N.Q.S.D., 20, 1930-32, p.124-7. [Includes names of mariners of Bristol & Somerset, 1570]

Members of a 'luxury' trade are identified in:

BELLCHAMBERS, Jack Kenneth. Somerset clockmakers. Antiquarian Horological Society monographs, 4. London: the Society, 1968.

The medical trades - physicians, dentists, and apothecaries - have been listed in:

COX, J. Stephen. 'Physicians of Dorset and Somerset, 1603-1643', N.Q.S.D., 28, 1968, p.198-200.

BROWN, P. S. 'Bath: dentists advertising in 18th c. Bath newspapers', N.Q.S.D., 30, 1974-9, p.278-82.

WHITTET, T. D. 'Somerset apothecaries' tokens and their issuers', S.A.N.H.S., 130, 1985/6, p.127-33.

A listing of present day Somerset authors is given in:

HANDLEY-TAYLOR, Geoffrey. Devon, Dorset, and Somerset authors today: being a checklist of authors born in these counties together with brief particulars of authors born elsewhere ... London: Eddison Press, 1973.

For musicians, see:

JEBOULT, Harold A. Somerset composers, musicians and music. Somerset folk series, 10. London: Somerset Folk Press, 1923. See also: JEBOULT, Harold A. 'Somerset composers and musicians', N.Q.S.D., 13, 1913, p.249-52. See also p.331, & 15, 1917, p.29.

The names of many freemasons are given in two works:

FISHER, Wilfred G. The history of the Provincial Grand Lodge of Somerset. [Bath?]: Provincial Grand Lodge of Somerset, 1962. [Biographical notes on provincial grand masters, 1768-1962; many other names]

Centenary history, 1810-1910: an epitome of 100 years masonic work of Lodge of Brotherly Love, no.329. Yeovil: W. Beale Collins, 1910. [Yeovil lodge; includes list of members 1810-1910, giving occupations and residences]

Many Somersetians have served in the army, and much information on them is contained in the many regimental histories which have been written. The list which follows is intended as a guide to those publications which contain lists of officers and men, and which therefore have genealogical value. It is arranged in chronological order. For muster rolls, etc., of the 16th & 17th centuries, see chapter 11.

EVERETT, Sir Henry. The history of the Somerset Light Infantry (Prince Albert's), 1685-1914. London: Methuen, 1934. [Includes biographical notes on the Colonels, 1685-1914, lists of Lieutenant-Colonels and adjutants, and many other names]

CARTER, Thomas. Historical record of the thirteenth, first Somersetshire, or Prince Albert's regiment of Light Infantry. London: W. O. Mitchell, 1867. [Includes biographical notices of Colonels, 1685-1864]

SMYTHIES, R. H. Raymond. Historical records of the 40th (2nd Somersetshire) regiment, now 1st Battalion the Prince of Wales's Volunteers (South Lancashire Regiment) from its formation in 1717 to 1893. Devonport: A. H. Swiss, 1894. [Includes various rolls of officers]

FISHER, W. G. The history of Somerset yeomanry, volunteer and territorial units. Taunton: Goodman & Sons, 1924. [1794-1923; gives names of captains and officers]

FORTESCUE-BRICKDALE, Sir Charles. 'Military subscriptions of the county of Somerset for internal defence, 1794', S.A.N.H.S., 79(2), 1933, p.95-100.

Soldiers died in the Great War, 1914-19. Part 18. Prince Albert's (Somerset Light Infantry). Polstead, Suffolk: J. B. Hayward & Son, 1989. Originally published 1920.

Somerset County War Memorial: report of administration of fund, order of dedication service, list of subscribers, roll of honour. Taunton: E. Goodman & Son, Phoenix Press, 1923.

BOYLE, R. C. A record of the West Somerset yeomanry, 1914-1919. London: St. Catherine Press, [192-?] [Includes roll of honour, etc.]

MAJENDIE, V. H. B. A history of the 1st Battalion, the Somerset Light Infantry (Prince Albert's) July 1st, 1916 to the end of the war. Taunton: Goodman & Son, 1921. [Includes lists of casualties and decorations]

WYRALL, Everard. The history of the Somerset Light Infantry (Prince Albert's), 1914-1919. London: Methuen, 1927. [Includes lists of honours, etc]

The story of no. 2 Company of the 7th Battn. Somerset Home Guard. Bristol: Bennet Bros., [194-?] [Includes nominal roll, 1944, etc.]

KERR, W. J. Records of the 1st Somerset militia (3rd Bn. Somerset L. I). Aldershot: Gale & Polden, 1930. [Includes roll of officers]

Two schools have published lists of their old boys who saw active service:

GRAHAM, Lucius. Downside: the war, 1914-1919, containing lists of old Gregorians who served in H. M. Forces during the war, together with memoirs of those killed in action or who died on active service. London: Hudson & Kearns, 1925.

TROTMAN, E. E. Record of war service, 1939-1945, compiled for the Old Brutonian Association. Taunton: Hammett & Co., [1947]

CHAPTER 6
VISITATION PEDIGREES, ETC

In the sixteenth and seventeenth centuries, the heralds undertook 'visitations' of the counties in order to determine the rights of gentry to bear heraldic arms. One consequence of this activity was the compilation of pedigrees of most of the leading gentry. These visitation returns continue to be major sources of genealogical information, and many have been published. See:

WEAVER, Frederic William, ed. The visitations of Somerset in the years 1531 and 1573, together with additional pedigrees chiefly from the visitation of 1591. Exeter: Pollard, 1885.

VIVIAN-NEAL, A. W. 'The visitations of Somerset, 1573, 1591: notes on Ralph Brooke's manuscript', S.A.N.H.S., 84(2), 1940, p.114-23.

COLBY, Frederick Thomas, ed. The visitation of the county of Somerset in the year 1623. Harleian Society visitations, 11. London: the Society, 1876.

See also:

BENSON, Robert, & VIVIAN-NEAL, A. W. 'The visitation of Somerset, 1623: notes on John Goff's manuscript', S.A.N.H.S., 90, 1944, p.82-101.

WERE, F. 'Notes and queries regarding the Heralds' return of parishes, hamlets or manors, entered under the headings of hundreds in Colby's Visitations of Somerset, p.132-46', N.Q.S.D., 90, 1905, p.80-3.

WEAVER, F. W. 'Somersetshire notes, heraldic and genealogical', S.A.N.H.S., 33(2), 1887, p.19-36. [General discussion of visitations]

The purpose of heraldic visitations was to determine who had the right to bear arms. Grants of arms are listed in:

JEWERS, A. J. 'Grants of arms to Somerset and Dorset families', N.Q.S.D., 4, 1894-5, p.149-55, 226-30, & 255-60. [16-17th c.]

An eighteenth century armory is discussed in:

VIVIAN-NEAL, A. W. 'Notes on an eighteenth century armory of Somerset', S.A.N.H.S., 85(2), 1939, p.134-50.

The most up to date survey of Somerset hatchments is:

SUMMERS, Peter, ed. Hatchments in Britain, v.7: Cornwall, Devon, Dorset, Gloucestershire, Hampshire, Isle of Wight and Somerset. London: Phillimore, 1988

Sigillography - the study of seals - may also be of value to the genealogist. See:

TREMLETT, T. D. 'Seals of some Somerset families during the middle ages', S.A.N.H.S., 94, 1948-9, p.92-8.

CHAPTER 7
FAMILY HISTORIES

A considerable amount of research on Somerset family history has been completed, and is listed here. This list includes published books and journal articles; it does not, however, include the innumerable notes and queries published in journals such as G.T. and N.Q.S.D., except where substantial information is provided. It also excludes studies which have not been published.

ABBOT

See Raymond

ADAMS

BARTLETT, J. Gardner. Henry Adams of Somersetshire, England and Braintree, Mass: his English ancestry and some of his descendants. New York: privately printed, 1927.

ALFORD

ALFORD, Josiah George. Alford family notes. London: Phillimore, 1908. [Includes will abstracts]

STANDERWICK, John Wm. 'Alford family of Co. Somerset', N.Q.S.D., 5, 1897-8, p.69-70. See also p.190 & 219.

AMES

AMES, Reginald. 'Pedigree of Ames', Genealogist, 2, 1878, p.273-81. [Of Somerset, Gloucestershire, Hertfordshire & London; 17-19th c.]

BACON

BARTLETT, R. G. 'Bacon family of Somerset', N.Q.S.D., 3, 1893, p.16. See also p.53. [Includes pedigree, 17-18th c.]

BOND, T. 'On the family of Roger Bacon', S.A.N.H.S., 25(2), 1879, p.29-32. [Medieval]

BADCOCK

TYLER, J. C. 'Badcock of Devon and Somerset', M.G.H., 5th series, 6, 1926-8, p.301-9. [Includes wills]

BAKER

BAKER, Gordon. Of Somerset stock: the fortunes of a country family. Williton: the author, 1980. [Baker family; includes pedigrees, 14-20th c.]

BALCH

BALCH, Galusha B. Genealogy of the Balch family in America. Salem, Mass: Eben Putnam, 1897. [Originally a Somerset family]

BALCH, J. 'Husbands and wives: Balch spouses', G.T., 13(3), 1988, p.88-9. [List of spouses, with dates of marriage]

BALCH, Thomas Wiling. Balch genealogica. Philadelphia: Allen, Lane & Scott, 1907. [Somerset & U.S. family]

BAMPFYLDE

HYLTON, Lord. 'The manor houses of Hardington and Vallis', S.A.N.H.S., 74, 1928, p.78-86.

BARNES

BARNES, Arthur Harman. History of a family: Barnes. [Ormskirk: the author?], 1967-8. [Of Frome, Bristol, Herefordshire & Reading, Berkshire; includes pedigrees, 17-20th c.]

BARROW

See Paulet

BAVE

POYNTON, F. J. 'Evidences from registers supporting the pedigree of Bave', M.G.H., 2nd series, 1, 1886, p.216-8. [Parish register extracts from Bath Abbey, St. James Bath, Tickenham, and St. James, Bristol]

POYNTON, F. J. 'The Baves of Bath and of Barrow Court, Tickenham, Co. Somerset, allied to the Haringtons, both of Kelston and Corston, in the same county', M.G.H., 2nd series, 1, 1886, p.167-70. [Includes monumental inscriptions from various churches]

POYNTON, F. J. 'Pedigree of Bave of Bath and of Barrow Court, Tickenham', M.G.H., 2nd series, 1886, p.189-92.

BAYLEY

HORTON-SMITH, L. Graham H. 'The Bayley family of Dorset, Somerset, Oxon, and Berks', N.Q.S.D., 25, 1950, p.41-9.

BEAUCHAMP

BATTEN, John. 'The barony of Beauchamp of Somerset', S.A.N.H.S., 36(2), 1890, p.20-59.

CARTER, W. F. 'The Beauchamps of Somerset', Genealogist, N.S., 33, 1916-17, p.151-4.

BELET

HARFIELD, C. G. 'The Belets: the Norman connection', N.Q.S.D., 32, 1986- , p.536-47. [General discussion]

BEVYN

See Montagu

BILBIE

BAILEY, R. 'Eccentric bell-founders of the Mendips', Country life, 125, 1959, p.212-3. [18th c., Bilbie family]

BIRCH

'Birch family in Somerset and Dorset', N.Q.S.D., 25, 1950, p.219-22. [Includes pedigree 17-18th c.]

BISSE

GRIGSON, F. 'Genealogical memoranda relating to the Bisse family', M.G.H., 2nd series, 1, 1886, p.322-4, 328-32, 342-5, 369-72, & 376-9; 2, 1888, p.12-15, 20-23, 62-4, 78-9, 93-4, 110-12, & 125-8. [Includes will extracts, Chancery proceedings, and parish register extracts from Milton Clevedon, Maperton, etc]

GRIGSON, F. 'Pedigree of Bisse', M.G.H., 2nd series, 2, 1888, p.139-52. [Includes extracts from Almsford, Martock, and other parish registers]

JEWERS, Arthur J. 'Bisse family', N.Q.S.D., 5, 1897-8, p.213-6. See also p.310. [Includes wills, monumental inscriptions and parish register extracts]

WIGAN, Herbert. 'Bisse notes: being additions to genealogical memoranda relating to the Bisse family compiled by Mr. Francis Grigson', M.G.H., 3rd series, 4, p.122-7. [Includes amended pedigree, list and some abstracts of Bisse wills; also wills of Thomas Ashe of Batcomb, 1558, & Mathewe Grene of Milton Clevedon, 1574]

'Bisse pedigree', M.G.H., 2nd series, 1, 1886, p.283-5.

BLAKE

CURTIS, C. D. 'Blake, Robert, General-at-Sea (1598-1657)', N.Q.S.D., 29, 1974, p.141-3, & 166-170.

SAYER, M. J. 'Pedigrees of county families', Genealogists' magazine, 19(8), 1978, p.285-6.

A record of the Blakes of Somersetshire, especially in the line of William Blake of Dorchester, Mass., the emigrant to New England, with one branch of his descendants. Boston: privately printed, 1881. [14-19th c.]

BOTREAUX

See Moeles

BRETT

BROWN, Frederick. 'The Brett family', S.A.N.H.S., 28(2), 1882, p.79-88.

BRIWES

GRIFFITH, L. 'Briwes of Staple, Somerset', Notes & queries, 162, 1932, 3-5, 21-4, 39-42, 59-61, 78-80, 95-7, 132-4, 164-5, 218-20, 254-6, 276-9, 311-13, 402-3, 416-8, 434-7 & 455-8. [13-14th c.]

BROOK

ROGERS, W. H. Hamilton. Brook of Somerset and Devon: barons of Cobham in the county of Kent, their local history and descent. Taunton: Barnicott and Pearce, 1899-1901. [Reprinted from S.A.N.H.S., 44(2), 1898, p.1-78, 45(2), 1899, p.1-24, & 46(2), 1900, p.109-24; also reprinted in his Archaeological papers relating to the counties of Somerset, Wilts., Hants., and Devon. [ ]: the author, 1902]

WERE, F. 'Brook family', N.Q.S.D., 6, 1899, p.263-4.

BULL

See Clarke

BURCIE

LYTE, H. C. Maxwell. 'Burcie, Falaise and Martin', S.A.N.H.S., 65(2), 1919, p.1-27.

BURLAND

B., J. B. H. 'The Burlands of Steyning', N.Q.S.D., 3, 1893, p.269. [Includes pedigree]

BURTON

BERESFORD, John. 'The Burtons of Sutton Montis, Co. Somerset', Notes & queries, 150, 1926, p.404-5.

BYFLEET

WHITFIELD, I. M. 'A Somerset recusant family', N.Q.S.D., 29, 1974, p.215-20. [Byfleet of Bratton Seymour, 16-17th c.]

CANYNGES

PRYCE, George. Memorials of the Canynges family and their times ... Bristol: John Wright for the author, 1854.

CAREW

'Armorial bookplate', M.G.H., N.S., 4, 1884, p.154. [of Camerton]

See also Craucombe

CARY

ROBINSON, Charles J. 'Cary family: arms in East Coker church', Herald & genealogist, 1865, p.341-4. [Includes pedigree, c.15-17th c.]

CHAFE

CHAFY, W. K. W. Gesta Chaforum, or, notes on, and diaries kept by, the Chafes or Chafys of Chafe-combe, Exeter, and Sherbourne. Rous Lench Court: privately printed, 1910.

CHAFFIN

DRAKE, Phyllis & DRAKE, Stella Judy. The Chaffin family: a study of one name. Basingstoke: the author, 1986.

CHASEY

CHASEY, Harold. 'The Chasey family of central Somerset', N.Q.S.D., 31, 1980-85, p.411-4.

CHEDDER

GEORGE, W. 'The De Chedder family of Bristol and Cheddar', S.A.N.H.S., 34(2), 1888, p.114-6. [13-14th c.]

CHENEY

BATTEN, John. 'The lady of Poyntington', S.A.N.H.S., 42(2), 1896, p.1-5. [Cheney family; includes pedigree, 13-15th c.]

CHESNEY

CHESNEY, R. W. L. 'Some medieval sheriffs of Somerset and Dorset', Genealogists' magazine, 17, 1973, p.315-20. [Chesney family]

CHETWYND

See Harington

CHIDGEY

GILMAN, J. M. 'Captain Thomas Chidgey and the port of Watchet', Maritime history, 4, 1974, p.31-48.

CHOKE

ROSENTHAL, Joel T. 'Sir Richard Choke (d.1483) of Long Ashton', S.A.N.H.S., 127, 1982/3, p.105-21. [Includes genealogical information]

CHURCHEY

SWEETMAN, George. The "Dogs" and its owners, with particular reference to the Churchey family in Wincanton. Yeovil: Western Printing & Publishing Co., [for the Wincanton Field Club], 1900.

CLARKE

JEWERS, A. J. 'Clarke family', N.Q.S.D., 5, 1897-8, p.274-6. [16th c.]

SUTTON, George Barry. A history of shoe making in Street, Somerset: C. & J. Clark, 1833-1903. York: William Sessions, 1979. [Includes pedigree showing linkage of Clark, Sturge, Melford, Bull & Stephens families, 17-20th c.]

CLAYFIELD-IRELAND

WILLIAMSON, B. The Clayfield-Irelands of Brislington. [ ]: [ ], 1986.

CLEVEDON

MACLEAN, Sir John. 'The Clevedon family', S.A.N.H.S., 41(2), 1895, p.1-37. [Includes pedigree, 11-15th c.]

See also Courtenay

COKER

WERE, F. 'Coker armorials', N.Q.S.D., 7, 1901, p.328-9. See also p.347.

COLLIER

See Dodington

COMPTON

'Comptons of Wigborough: baptisms of the Comptons of Wigborough and their connections in the registers of South Petherton, Co. Somerset', M.G.H., N.S., 4, 1884, p.334-5.

COPE

COPE, E. E. 'Pedigree of the family of Cope', M.G.H., 3rd series, 4, 1902, p.237-44 & 289-91.

CORBEN

DAVIS, F. N. 'Corben family', N.Q.S.D., 18, 1926, p.139-40.

COTTELL

COTTELL, William Henry. A history of the Cotel, Cottell, or Cottle family, of the counties of Devon, Somerset, Cornwall and Wilts., compiled from county histories, heralds visitations, etc. London: Taylor & Co., 1871.

COTTELL, W. H. 'Cotel, Cottell, or Cottle family', N.Q.S.D., 1, 1890, p.105-6. [Includes grant of free warren to Sir Edye Cotel, Knt., 1248, with names of witnesses]

COTTELL, William Henry. Pedigree of the family of Cotell, Cotele, Cottell, or Cottle of the counties of Devon, Somerset, Cornwall, and Wilts. London: Mitchell & Hughes, [1891]

COURTENAY

ROGERS, W. H. Hamilton. 'Courtenay-Clyvedon, in Somerset', N.Q.S.D., 6, 1899, p.241-5. [Reprinted in his Archaeological papers relating to the counties of Somerset, Wilts., Hants., and Devon. [ ]: reprinted for the author, 1902]

See also Engayne & Rogers

COX

COX, A. F. W. 'Cox families of the West of England', Devon and Cornwall notes and queries., 22(18), 1946, p.327-8. [Of Devon, Dorset and Somerset]

COX, A. F. Warburton. 'Cox of the West of England', N.Q.S.D., 24, 1946, p.289-92.

CRAUCOMBE

BATTEN, John. 'Craucombe-Carew', N.Q.S.D., 6, 1899, p.49-56.

CROCKER

CROCKER, W. T. The Crockers of Ashcombe Farm. Canberra: Summit Press, 1979. [Includes pedigree, 18-20th c.]

CROOM

See Gostlett

CRUTTWELL

CRUTTWELL, Harry Athill. The chronicle of Crotall, Cruthal, Cruttall or Cruttwell and Bath. [ ]: Camberley, Hickmott & Co., 1933. [Of Wokingham, Berkshire, and Bath]

CURCI

LYTE, Sir Henry C. Maxwell. 'Curci', S.A.N.H.S., 66(2), 1920, p.98-126.

DACKOMBE

FRY, E. A. 'Templecombe register: Dackombe family', N.Q.S.D., 5, 1897-8, p.133.

DALISON

See Walker

DALLIMORE

McGARVIE, Michael. 'The Dallimores of Nunney', N.Q.S.D., 30, 1974-9, p.107-10. [16-19th c.]

DAMPIER

W., W. 'Dampier of East Coker', Notes & queries, 154, 1928, p.17. See also p.195-6 & 227-8.

DANEYS

DENNY, Henry L. L. 'Notes on the family of Le Daneys', N.Q.S.D., 21, 1935, 39-42, 73-7 & 127-8.

DAUBENEY

DAUBENEY, Giles. The history of the Daubeney family. Pontypool: Griffin Press, 1951.

See also Engayne

DE HAVILAND

[DE HAVILAND, John Von Sonntag]. Chronicle of the ancient and noble Norman family of De Haviland, originally of Haverland, in the Cotentin, Normandy, now of Guernsey, including the English branches of Havelland of Dorsetshire, now extinct, Haviland of Hawkesbury, Goucestershire, also extinct, and Haviland of Somerset-shire, with the documentary evidence. St. Louis: Mekeel Press, 1895.

DENYS

BUSH, Thomas S. 'The Denys family and their connections with the manors of Alveston, Siston and Dyrham', Proceedings of the Bath Natural History and Antiquarian Field Club, 9, 1901, p.58-70. [Includes wills, inquisitions post mortem & pedigree, 15-16th c.]

DICKINSON

BURDEN, Joy. *Winging Westward: from Eton dungeon to Millfield desk*. Bath: Robert Wall Books, 1974. [Dickinson of King Weston; includes pedigree, 16-20th c.]

DIGGES

See Harington

DODDERIDGE

'Pedigree of Dodderidge of Crowcombe, Co. Somerset', *M.G.H.*, 4th series, 5, 1914, p.293-7.

DODDERIDGE, Sidney E. 'Dudderidge alias Dodderidge of Devon, Somerset and Dorset', *N.Q.S.D.*, 9, 1905, p.157-65. See also 13, 1913, p.328-30.

DODDERIDGE, Sydney E. 'Dodderidge of Stogumber, Co. Somerset', *N.Q.S.D.*, 14, 1915, p.19-22. [16-18th c.]

DODDERIDGE, S. E. 'Pedigrees of Dodderidge', *M.G.H.*, 5th series, 1, 1916, p.68-72, 146-52, 195-8, 236-8, & 274-5. Addenda, 3, 1918-19, p.127.

'Dodderidge of Dotheridge, Co. Devon, and Crowcombe, Co. Somerset', *M.G.H.*, 4th series, 5, 1914, p.261-4.

DODINGTON

'Pedigree of Dodington, from visitations of Somerset, 1623', *Genealogist*, 1, 1877, p.23-8. See also p.29 & 155-6.

COOPER, T. 'The families of Dodington and Collier', *Topographer & genealogist*, 3, 1858, p.568-75.

MARSHALL, George W. 'Genealogical notices of the family of Dodington, Somerset', *Reliquary*, p.86-90.

See also Marriott

DOONE

RAWLE, Edwin John. *The Doones of Exmoor*. London: Thomas Burleigh; Taunton: Barnicott & Pearce, 1903.

THORNYCROFT, L. B. *The story of the Doones in fact, fiction and photo*. 3rd ed. Taunton: Barnicotts, 1947.

DOWLING

GOULD, Kenneth J. 'The Dowlings of Somerset and Michigan', *G.T.*, 5(2), 1980, p.12-13.

DRURY

See Willis

DUCKWORTH

McGARVIE, M. 'The Duckworths and the building of Orchardleigh House', *Ancient Monuments Society Tr.*, 27, 1983, p.119-45.

DUMMER

'Pedigree of Dummer of Penne Domer, Co. Somerset, and of Dummer, Co. Hants', *S.A.N.H.S.*, 17, 1871, p.114-5. [12-17th c.]

DWELLY

DWELLY, E. *Compendium of notes on the Dwelly family*. Fleet: the author, 1912.

DYER

DYER, A. O. 'Dyer of Wincanton and Roundhill', *N.Q.S.D.*, 28, 1968, p.185-6.

MARTIN, E. H. 'Dyer family', *N.Q.S.D.*, 10, 1907, p.97-107, & 145-57. See also 10, 1907, p.170, & 11, 1909, p.177. [15-17th c.]

See also Swinnerton

DYKE

PAINTER, G. C. 'Dyke family of West Somerset', *N.Q.S.D.*, 7, 1901, p.192-6. See also p.267-8 & 319-20.

EASTON

'The family of Easton, of Morchard Episcopi, Devon, and Bradford, Somerset', Western antiquary, 6(5), 1886, p.125-9. See also p.166-7, 169-70, 250, & 272-3. [Medieval]

EDWARDS

SKINNER, A. J. P. 'West Country families: Edwards', N.Q.S.D., 15, 1917, p.243-5. [Of Dorset, Somerset and Devon; 17-19th c.]

ELKINGTON

ELKINGTON, Arthur Edward Hardwicke, & ELKINGTON, Christine Mary. The Elkingtons of Bath, being the ancestry and descendants of George Elkington of Bath (1566-1640). Woodstock, Oxon: the author, 1959.

ENGAYNE

R., W. H. H. 'The Pabenham brass, Offord D'Arcy church, Huntingdon', N.Q.S.D., 10, 1907, p.241-2. See also p.301-2. [Engayne, Pabenham, Courtenay & Daubeney families]

ENGLAND

See Phillips

FALAISE

See Burcie

FANE

CAREW, Joyce. Dusty pages: a story of two families and their homes. Bridport: C. J. Creed, 1971. [Fane & Fortescue families of Dorset, Devon, Somerset & Hampshire]

FITZJAMES

BROWN, Frederick. 'On the family of Fitzjames', S.A.N.H.S., 24(2), 1878, p.32-42.

MAYO, C. H. 'The Fitzjames family of Somerset and later of Dorset', N.Q.S.D., 16, 1920, p.54-68, 88-100, 128-38, 179-87, 218-27 & 247-55. [14-18th c.]

HUMPHREYS, A. L., & WAINEWRIGHT, J. B.

'Fitzjames', Notes & queries, 11th series, 12, 1915, p.202-4. See also p.100.

FLOWER

FLOWER, N. L. 'The Flower family of Somerset', N.Q.S.D., 29, 1974, p.277-9. [16-20th c.]

FORTESCUE

See Fane

FOX

FOX, Charles H. Chronicles of Tonedale: two centuries of family history. Taunton: Barnicott & Son, 1879. [Fox family, 18-19th c.]

FOX, Hubert. Quaker broadcloth: the story of Joseph and Mariana Fox and the cousinry at Wellington. Buckfastleigh: the author, 1981.

See also Were

FREKE

FREKE, Ralph, et al. '[Pedigree of Freke]', Ancestor, 10, 1904, p.179-212, & 11, 1904, p.33.

FRY

FRY, Edward Alexander. 'Fry of Yarty', S.A.N.H.S., 49(2), 1903, p.65-70.

FRY, George S. 'Fry of Glastonbury', N.Q.S.D., 19, 1929, 69-71. [Includes 15th c. pedigree.]

FULLER

FULLER, J. F. 'Fuller of Bath', M.G.H., 5th series, 1916, p.137-43.

FURNEAUX

FURNEAUX, H. 'Notices of the family of Furneaux from the eleventh to the fifteenth century', M.G.H., 3rd series, 3, 1900, p.272-6. [Pedigree]

LYTE, H. Maxwell. 'The co-heirs of Furneaux', N.Q.S.D., 16, 1920, p.281-5.

'Descendants of Matthew Furneaux', Collectanea topographica et genealogica, 1, 1834, p.243-8. [Medieval]

FUSSELL

ATTHILL, R. 'A dynasty of ironmasters', Country life, 131, 1962, p.1254-9. [Fussell and Horner families]

GIBBES

ALDENHAM, Lord. Pedigree of the family of Gibbs, of Clyst St. George, Co. Devon, Aldenham, Co. Hertford, Tyntesfield, Charlton, and Barrow Court, Co. Somerset. London: privately printed, 1904.

GIBBS, Henry Hucks. 'Pedigree of Gibbes of Bedminster and Bristol, allied to Harington of Kelston, Somerset', M.G.H., 2nd series, 1, 1886, p.3-6.

GILLARD

GILLARD, Jeffrey J. Thick on the ground. Melbourne: the author, 1978. [Of Somerset & Australia]

GILLING

G., A. H. 'A Somerset yeoman family', N.Q.S.D., 10, 1907, p.72-6. [Gilling of South Brent, 14-20th c.]

GODDARD

See Harington

GODOLPHIN

MARSH, F. G. The Godolphins. New Milton: Smith & Son, 1930.

GOLDE

ROGERS, W. H. Hamilton. 'Golde-Strechleigh of Seaborough, Somerset, and Ermington, South Devon', N.Q.S.D., 7, 1901, p.91-8. [Reprinted in his Archaeological papers relating to the counties of Somerset, Wilts., Hants., and Devon. [ ]: reprinted for the author, 1902.

GOODHINDS

GOULSTONE, J. The Goodhinds of Saltford: notes, wills and pedigrees. [Bexleyheath]: the author, 1985.

GORGES

BROWN, Frederick. 'Pedigree of Sir Ferdinando Gorges', New England historical and genealogical register., 1875, p.7-11. [Of Wraxall, 16-18th c.]

GORGES, Raymond. The story of a family through eleven centuries, illustrated by portraits and pedigrees, being a history of the family of Gorges. Boston: Merrymount Press, 1944.

GOSTLETT

POYNTON, F. J. 'Gostlett of Marshfield, allied to Harington of Kelston', M.G.H., N.S., 4, 1884, p.2-4. [Includes extracts from Kelston parish register and monumental inscriptions for Croom family, and a pedigree of Harington of Bitton, Gloucestershire]

GRENE

See Bisse

GROVE

See Hanham

GYVERNEY

HARBIN, E. H. Bates. 'Walter Fichet's grant of lands to Simon Michel, circa 1300', S.A.N.H.S., 64(2), 1918, p.46-60. [Includes pedigrees of Gyverney, 12-14th c., & Michel, 13-17th c.]

HANCOCK

HANCOCK, F. Hancock of Somerset: some notes on a yeoman family. Taunton: Barnicott & Pearce, 1919.

HANHAM

HAWKINS, Desmond. 'Hanham and Grove families', N.Q.S.D., 31, 1980-85, p.243-4.

HARBIN

RAWLINS, Sophia W. 'Joseph and Alexander Harbin: two Barbadian merchants, their families and descendants', Journal of the Barbados Museum and Historical Society, 11(1), 1951, p.28-33. [Somerset family; 17th c.]

HARDING

REID, R. D. Some account of the Harding family of Cranmore, Co. Somerset, together with notes on the Yeoman family of Wanstrow. Bristol: J. W. Arrowsmith, 1917.

ROYAL, Nicholas John. Harding family: a short history and narrative pedigree from 1480 to the present day. [ ]: privately printed, 1970.

HARINGTON

'A brief account of the complaint made by Sir John Harington of Kelston, kt., to the Star Chamber, against his brother-in-law Edward Rogers of Cannington, Somerset', M.G.H., N.S., 4, 1884, p.261.

'A brief memoir and some other notes of John Harington of Kelston, M.P. for Bath, 1464-54-56', M.G.H., N.S., 3, 1880, p.398-401.

'Extracts from the registers of the parishes of Kelston and Corston, Somerset, and from Bitton in Gloucestershire, relating to the family of Harington', M.G.H., N.S., 3, 1880, p.194-7.

'Genealogical table showing the descent of Harington of Somerset from the reign of Henry VIII to A. D. 1700 ... ', M.G.H., N.S., 4, 1884, p.190-6.

'The genealogy of Harington of Kelston, Co. Somerset, resumed from A. D. 1700', M.G.H., N.S., 4, 1884, p.366-7.

'Grant of arms to John Harington of Kelston, 1568', M.G.H., N.S., 3, 1880, p.17-19. [Includes a memoir of John Harington]

'Harington of Corston in the county of Somerset', M.G.H., N.S., 4, 1884, p.274-7.

'The Haringtons of North Devon, descending from those of Somerset', M.G.H., N.S., 3, 1880, p.333 & 346-8. [Includes entries from parish register of Shebbear, North Devon]

'Harington of Somerset, and Chetwynd of Ingestre, Staffordshire', M.G.H., N.S., 3, 1880, p.316-8.

'A memoir of Captain John Harington of Corston and Kelston, Somerset, M.P. for Somerset, 1654, M.P. for Bath city, 1658', M.G.H., N.S., 4, 1884, p.22-4.

'Pedigree of Harington of Corston', M.G.H., N.S., 4, 1884, p.291-6 & 378-83.

The pedigree of the Harrington family (reprinted from an ancient book). London: Mitre Press, [195-?] [Extracts from parish registers]

'The political jeopardy of John Harington, esq., in 1660, and by what friends he was rescued from it', M.G.H., N.S., 4, 1884, p.33-6.

GRIMBLE, Ian. The Harington family. London: Jonathan Cape, 1957.

MORE, J. H. 'Family portraits: only a name', Listener, 6.9.1956, p.336-8.

POYNTON, F. J. 'The last days of Harington at Kelston', M.G.H., 2nd series, 1, 1886, p.316-8 & 338-40.

POYNTON, F. J. 'Pedigrees showing the connection of Harington of Kelston, Somerset, with the Wiltshire families of Digges, Thorner, Goddard, and White', M.G.H., 2nd series, 1, 1886, p.37-40.

POYNTON, Francis J. 'Who was Margaret, wife of William, V Lord Harington, 1418?', Genealogist, N.S., 9, 1893, p.78. [Includes will of Robert Hylle of Spaxton, Somerset]

See also Bave, Gibbes, Gostlett, Horner & Rogers

HARRISON

'Extracts from the parish register of West Quantoxhead, Co. Somerset, relating to the family of Harison', Genealogist, 2, 1878, p.24-6.

HAVILAND

See De Haviland

HAWKER

OGGINS, Virginia D., & Robin S. 'Some Hawkers of Somerset', S.A.N.H.S., 124, 1979/80, p.51-60. [11-13th c.]

HAWLEY

S. 'Does an heir to the Barony of Hawley exist?', Genealogist, 1, 1877, p.161-3. [17-18th c.]

HEAL

HEAL, Ambrose, & HEAL, Edith. The records of the Heal family. [   ]: privately printed, 1932. [Includes monumental inscriptions, parish register extracts, wills, etc]

HEYRON

KRAUSS, Russell. 'John Heyron of Newton Plecy, Somerset', Speculum, 10(2), 1935, p.187-9. [14th c.]

HIPPISLEY

JONES, I. Fitzroy. 'Sir John Cox Hipisley', Genealogists' magazine, 6(11), 1934, p.505-6.

HIPPISLEY-SEAMAN

JEBOULT, Edward. The Hippisley-Seaman family of Shiplette Manor, Bleadon, Somerset. [Taunton?]: [the author?], 1891.

See also Seaman

HOBHOUSE

HOBHOUSE, Sir Charles Percy. Some account of the family of Hobhouse and reminiscences. Leicester: Johnson Wykes & Co., 1909. [Includes pedigree, 18-20th c.]

HOBHOUSE, Henry. Hobhouse memoirs. Taunton: Barnicott & Pearce, 1927. [14-20th c.]

HODY

DILKS, T. Bruce. 'The Hody family', N.Q.S.D., 24, 1946, p.22-5. [15th c.]

HOOD

BARTELOT, R. G. 'The naval Hoods of Dorset and Somerset', N.Q.S.D., 17, 1923, p.23-9.

HOOPER

See Rawlins

HOPTON

RUTTON, W. L. 'Pedigree of Hopton of Suffolk and Somerset', M.G.H., 3rd series, 3, 1900, p.9-12, 49-53, & 81-6.

HORNER

'Family of Horner, Co. Somerset, which a daughter of this house Capt. Harington of Corston and Kelston, C. Somerset, secondly inter-married', M.G.H., N.S., 4, 1884, p.160-4.

See also Fussell

HORSEY

BATTEN, John. 'The Horsey family', S.A.N.H.S., 43(2), 1897, p.84-93.

HOW

See Phillipps

HUDDESFIELD

See Rogers

HUNGERFORD

See Molyns

HUYSHE

ROGERS, W. H. Hamilton. 'Huyshe of Somerset and Devon: a pedigree', in his Archaeological papers relating to the counties of Somerset, Wilts, Hants and Devon. [ ]: the author, 1902. Reprinted from S.A.N.H.S., 43, 1897, p.1-44. [12-19th c.]

HYLLE

See Harington

IRELAND

See Clayfield-Ireland

ISHAM

LONGDEN, H. I. 'Isham family of Somerset', N.Q.S.D., 1, 1890, p.110-11. See also p.139-40. [17th c.]

LONGDEN, H. I. 'Isham family of Somerset', N.Q.S.D., 2, 1891, p.317-8.

LONGDEN, H. I. 'Isham family of Somerset', N.Q.S.D., 3, 1893, p.126-30. [Includes wills of William Isham of Bodrugan, Cornwall, 1572, Thomas Isham, 1588, & Roger Isham, 1653, both of Bradon, Ilbruers, John Isham of Langport-Eastover, 1675, & parish register entries from Edmonton, Middlesex]

LONGDEN, H. I. 'Isham family of Somerset', N.Q.S.D., 3, 1893, p.221-3.

JACKSON

See Raymond

JACOB

JACOB, Henry W. A history of the families of Jacob of Bridgwater, Tiverton and Southern Ireland. Taunton: Wessex Press, 1929.

JENNINGS

See Knight

KEYNES

GIBBON, R. G. 'The Keynes family in Somerset and Dorset', N.Q.S.D., 30, 1974-79, p.104-5.

KING

'Memoranda relating to the family of King, Castle Cary registers (Somerset)', M.G.H., N.S., 4, 1884, p.346-50.

KING, Edwin James. Records of the family of King, formerly of Leigh-upon-Mendip, Somerset. London: privately printed, 1937.

POOLE, H. J. 'King entries in the Stowell register', N.Q.S.D., 3, 1893, p.260-1.

KIRTON

REID, R. D. 'A local fragment', Somerset year book, 37, 1938, p.98-102. [Kirton family; includes pedigree, 18-19th c.]

KNIGHT

HALL, I. V. 'The connexions between John Knight, jnr., and the Parsons and Jennings families, 1641-79', Transactions of the Bristol & Gloucestershire Archaeological Society, 70, 1951, p.119-25.

LANE

JONES, I. Fitzroy. 'Note: John Lane, Chancellor of Lichfield', S.A.N.H.S., 93, 1947, p.135-6. [Notes on several 15th c. Somerset clergymen of this name]

LANGTON

DAVIS, Graham P. The Langtons at Newton Park. Bath: Fyson & Co., 1976. [Includes pedigree, 17-19th c.]

LAVOR

PITMAN, H. A. 'Henry Pitman, chirurgeon to the Duke of Monmouth', N.Q.S.D.,21, 1935, p.104-6. [Includes pedigree of Lavor, 17th c.]

LAWRENCE
'Lawrence pedigree from the visitation of the county of Somerset, 1623', M.G.H, 1, 1868, p.203.

See also Paulet

LEGG

MONK, Muriel. 'The Leggs of Sandford Orcas', G.T., 15(3), 1990, p.89. [Pedigree, 18-20th c.]

LEIR

'The Priory, Ditcheat, Somerset: a family and architectural history', Transactions of the Ancient Monuments Society, N.S., 24, 1980, p.75-125. [Home of the Leir family, 18-20th c.]

LETHBRIDGE

Royal descents of Sir John Hesketh Lethbridge, of Sandhill Park, Co. Somerset. London: John Camden Hotten, 1871.

LEVERSAGE

See Bampfylde

LINLEY

BLACK, Clementina. The Linleys of Bath. New ed. London: M. Secker, 1926. Reprinted London: Frederick Muller, 1971.

LISLE

NORRIS, H. 'George Lisle of Compton D'Urville', N.Q.S.D., 3, 1893, p.84-8. [Includes genealogical information]

LOCKETT

LOCKETT, R. Cyril. 'Family of Lockett', N.Q.S.D., 90, 1905, p.61-5. See also p.114. [Of Somerset, Dorset, Devon, and Cornwall]

LODERS

EAGERS, K. 'The Loders', G.T., 13(2), 1988, p.47.

LONG

'Long of Semington, Trowbridge, Whaddon, Monkton, &c., Co. Wilts; Beckington, Stratton and Downside, Co. Somerset', M.G.H., N.S., 3, 1880, p.396 (insert)

LOVEL

BAIN, J. 'The Lovels of Castle Cary and Hawick', Genealogist, N.S., 4, 1887, p.214-5.

LANDON, L. 'The Lovels of Castle Cary', N.Q.S.D., 18, 1926, p.173-6. [12th c.]

LUTTRELL

See Mohun

LYONS

PAUL, Roland W. 'The arms of Lyons of Long Ashton, Somerset', Proceedings of the Clifton Antiquarian Club, 6, 1908, p.208-15.

LYTE

LYTE, H. C. Maxwell. The Lytes of Lytescary. Taunton: Barnicott & Pearce, 1895. Reprinted from S.A.N.H.S., 38(2), 1892, p.1-100. For Supplement, see 77(2), 1931, p.115-35. [Includes pedigree]

McADAM

HALL, R. de Z. 'John Loudon McAdam and his descendents in Somerset', N.Q.S.D., 27, 1961, p.258-61.

MALET

BATTEN, J. 'Malet of Enmore, Somerset', N.Q.S.D., 3, 1893, p.255-8. [Primarily medieval deeds]

MALET, Arthur. 'Notes on the Malet family', S.A.N.H.S., 30(2), 1884, p.74-5. [12th c.]

MALET, Arthur. Notices of an English branch of the Malet family, compiled from family papers and other authentic sources. London: Harrison & Sons, 1885.

MALET, G. E. G. 'The origin of the Malets of Enmore', Genealogists' magazine, 8(6), 1939, p.316-24.

MALLET, Matilde. 'Origin of the name of Mallet and various ways of writing it', N.Q.S.D., 21, 1935, 51-4. See also p.83.

MARSHALL, G. W. 'The Malets of St. Audries', S.A.N.H.S., 16(2), 1870, p.35-40. [Includes pedigree, 14-17th c., & parish register extracts]

MARISCO

BROOKS, E. St John. 'The family of Marisco', Journal of the Royal Society of Antiquaries of Ireland, 61, 1931, p.22-38 & 89-112. [Of Lundy Island, Somerset, and Ireland]

MARRIOTT-DODINGTON

MARSHALL, G. W. 'Pedigree of Marriott-Dodington of Horsington', Reliquary, 13, 1872-3, p.244-5. [17-19th c.]

'Pedigree of Marriott-Dodington of Horsington', Genealogist, 1, 1877, p.81-4.

MARTIN

WATSON, W. G. Willis. The house of Martin: being chapters in the history of the West of England branch of that family. Exeter: William Pollard, 1906.

WILLIAMS, M. 'Genealogical memoranda relating to the Martyn family', M.G.H., N.S., 1, 1874, p.385-96. [Includes pedigrees, wills, parish register extracts, etc]

See also Burcie

MELFORD

See Clarke

MERIET

GREENFIELD, B. W. Genealogy of the Somersetshire family of Meriet ... Taunton: J. F. Hammond, 1883. [Reprinted from S.A.N.H.S., 28(2), 1882, p.99-215. Includes pedigree, 11-15th c.]

MERRICK

MERRICK, D. 'Merrick: my roots were built in Somerset', G.T., 13(4), 1988, p.134.

MICHELL

MICHELL, George B. 'Michell of Cannington', S.A.N.H.S., 73, 1927, p.80-5. [15-17th c.]

See also Gyverney

MIDELNEY

ROSS, D. Melville. 'Sir Ralph de Midelney', S.A.N.H.S. 61, 1916, p.143-56.

MILBORNE

MILBOURN, T. 'The family of Milborne of Somerset and Monmouthshire', M.G.H, 5th series, 3, 1918-19, p.13-40, 197-203, 235-44; 4, 1920-22, p.22-5, 45-51, 63-9, 91-4, 113-6, 137-8,165-78, 192-6, & 220-28.

MOELES

ROGERS, W. H. H. 'Lady Alice de Moels of North Cadbury', N.Q.S.D., 7, 1901, p.49-55. For pedigree, see also p.126-7

ROGERS, W. H. H. 'Moeles-Botreaux of North Cadbury, Somerset', N.Q.S.D., 6, 1899, p.289-95. See also p.359 & 7, 1901, p.21-2, 63-4, 127, & 142-3. [Medieval]

[Both the foregoing papers are reprinted in Rogers's Archaeological papers relating to the counties of Somerset, Wilts., Hants., and Devon. [ ]: the author, 1902]

MOHUN

LYTE, H. C. Maxwell. Dunster and its lords, 1066-1881. Exeter: W. Pollard, 1882.

LYTE, Sir H. C. A history of Dunster and the families of Mohun and Luttrell. 2 vols. London: St. Catherine's Press, 1909.

MOLYNS

ROGERS, W. H. H. 'Molyns-Hungerford, of Farleigh Hungerford, Somerset', N.Q.S.D., 6, 1899, p.337-43. See also 7, 1901, p.22-3. [Reprinted in Rogers's Archaeological papers relating to the counties of Somerset, Wilts., Hants., and Devon. [ ]: reprinted for the author, 1902; medieval]

MONTAGU

'Montagu of Sutton Montagu, Bevyn of Lufton, Muttlebury of Ashill in Ilminster, Smith of Thornecombe, Devon', N.Q.S.D., 20, 1930-2, p.18-19, 40-42, & 75-8.

MUCHGROS

HOUGHTON, F. T. S. 'Family of Muchgros', Birmingham Archaeological Society transactions, 47, 1921, p.8-34. [11-13th c; of Gloucestershire, Somerset, & various other counties]

MUSGRAVE

BARTLETT, R. G. 'Family of Musgrave', N.Q.S.D., 6, 1899, p.66-9. [16-17th c.]

MUTTLEBURY

See Montagu

NASHE

NORRIS, H. 'James Nashe', N.Q.S.D., 3, 1893, p.179. [Includes 17th c. pedigree]

NORRIS

DANIEL-TYSSEN, J. R. 'Norris pedigree', M.G.H., N.S., 1, 1874, p.101-3.

NOTCUTT

NOTCUTT, Michael Edward, & SARTIN, Marian Phyllis. The Notcutt family history, 1515-1989. Chatham: Backman & Turner, 1989. [Somerset, Essex & Suffolk]

NUTCOMBE

MONDAY, A. J. 'Clayhanger, in the county of Devon, and Raddington, in the county of Somerset', Western antiquary, 3, 1884, p.98-9. [Descent of Nutcombe family]

OATEN

OATEN, Edward F. 'Longevity in a Pitminster family', N.Q.S.D., 28, 1968, p.110-12.

OLDMIXON

ROGERS, P. 'Two notes on John Oldmixon and his family', Notes & queries, 17, 1970, p.293-300.

ORCHARD

VIVIAN-NEAL, A. W. 'Materials for the history of Orchard Portman', S.A.N.H.S., 89, 1943, p.35-53. [Includes pedigree of Orchard, 12-15th c.]

PABENHAM

See Engayne

PARDEE

JACOBS, Donald Lines, ed. The Pardee genealogy. New Haven: New Haven Colony Historical Society, 1927. [Of Somerset and New Haven; includes extracts from parish registers, wills, etc.]

PARKER

PARKER, Edward Milward Seede. Genealogical memoranda relating to the family of Parker, of Upton House, Upton Cheyney Manor, Bitton, Gloucestershire, and Welford House, Keynsham, Somerset; of Henbury, Clifton, Bristol, London and elsewhere, from 1543 to 1898. Bristol: Lavars & Co., 1899.

See also Paulet

PARSONS

See Knight

PAULET

FRANKLYN, Charles A. H. A genealogical history of the families of Paulet (or Pawlett), Berewe (or Barrow), Lawrence, and Parker ... Bedford: Foundry Press, 1963. [Paulet of Somerset and Gloucestershire; Barrow of Gloucestershire, Lawrence of Lancashire & Gloucestershire; Parker of Glamorganshire & Monmouthshire]

PAULL

PAUL, Henry N. Joseph Paull of Ilminster, Somerset, and some of his descendants who have resided in Philadelphia, Penns. Philadelphia: the author, 1932.

PENNY

EURE. 'Penny family', N.Q.S.D., 3, 1893, p.288.

PENNY, Frank. 'Penny family of Yeovil and Weymouth', N.Q.S.D., 15, 1917, p.61-3. [17-19th c.]

PENNY, Frank. 'Penne of East Coker, Somerset, and Toller Whelme, Dorset', N.Q.S.D., 10, 1907, p.12-17 & 53-9. [14-18th c.]

PEPPIN

PUGSLEY, Steven. The sturdy breed: the story of the Peppins of Dulverton and the development of the merino sheep. Zeal, Somerset: Hawkridge Press, 1988. [Australian pioneer family from Dulverton]

PERRETT

PERRETT, G. E. In search of the Perretts: a family history and genealogical survey. Bath: the author, 1983.

PHELIPS

PHELIPS, J. H. C. 'Phelips of Montacute: two early representatives', N.Q.S.D., 31, 1980-85, p.85-95. [15-16th c.]

PHELPS

PHELPS, Ron. 'Phelps brides and their grooms', G.T., 12(3), 1987, p.82-3. [Lists men marrying Phelps brides, with parishes and dates. See also 'Phelps grooms and their brides', G.T., 15(3), 1990, p.100-101.]

PHILLIPPS

SKINNER, A. J. P. 'Humphrey Phillipps', N.Q.S.D., 12, 1911, p.224-7. [Lists descendants, 17-19th c., including England and How families]

PITMAN

See Lavor

PLUMLEY

CURTIS, C. D. 'Monmouth rebellion: the Plumleys of Locking and Locking manor', N.Q.S.D., 29, 1974, p.269-72. See also 30, 1980, p.290-2.

POPHAM

POPHAM, Frederick W. A West country family: the Pophams from 1150. Sevenoaks: the author, 1976. [Somerset, Devon and Hampshire]

PORTMAN

HAWKINS, M. J. 'Wardship, royalist delinquency and too many children: the Portmans in the seventeenth century', Southern history, 4, 1982, p.55-89.

POWELL

CONNER, Phillip S. P. 'Somerset knighthood compositions', N.Q.S.D., 4, 1895, p.181. See also 5, 1897-8, p.273-4 & 317-8. [Powell family]

POWLETT

WINN, Colin G. The Powletts of Hinton St. George. London: Research Publishing, 1976.

PROWSE

WADE, E. F. 'Notes on the family of Prowse, of Compton Bishop, Co. Somerset', M.G.H., N.S., 3, 1880, p.162-3 & 165-9.

PYM

'An unpublished pedigree of Pym, from the original parchment roll', Genealogical magazine, 2, 1898-9, p.361-4.

CROUCH, W. 'Notes on the pedigree of Pym of Brymore, 1643', Genealogical magazine, 2, 1898-9, p.475-7.

PYNE

DODDERIDGE, Sidney E. 'Pyne of Edington, Co. Somerset', N.Q.S.D., 16, 1920, p.229-31. See also 23, 1942, p.240-2 & 252-3.

DODDERIDGE, Sidney E. 'Pyne of Stawell', N.Q.S.D., 17, 1923, p.248-9.

RALEGH

See Trevelyan

RAWLE

RAWLE, Edwin John. Records of the Rawle family, collected from the national archives, parish registers, wills and other sources. Taunton: Barnicott and Pearce, 1898.

RAWLINS

RAWLINS, Cosmo W. H. Family quartette: the families of Rawlins of Stoke Courcy (Somerset); Hooper of Devonport and Maidstone; Smith-Wyndham of E. Yorks, and Russell (Dukes of Bedford). Yeovil: the author, 1962. [Rawlins family, 19-20th c.]

RAYMOND

RAYMOND, John Marshall. Raymond, Abbot, Jackson and allied families. Palo Alto: Runnymede Press, 1962. [Primarily American, but includes pedigree of Raymond of Somerset & Dorset, 16-17th c.]

RENDALL

DAVIES, I. R. 'Charles Rendall, blacksmith', G.T., 13(2 & 3), 1988, p.49 & 79. [Crewkerne area]

HALL, R. de Z. 'Rendells of West Coker', N.Q.S.D., 28, 1968, p.265-7. [17-20th c.]

RETTER

STANES, R. 'Retter: the making of a surname', Devon & Cornwall notes & queries, 33(4), 1975, p.124-5. [Of East Devon and West Somerset, c.18th c.]

REYNOLDS

R., C. B. 'Reynolds family', N.Q.S.D., 11, 1909, p.23-4. [17-18th c.]

REYNY

LYTE, H. Maxwell. 'The heirs of Sir William de Reyny', N.Q.S.D., 19, 1929, p.52-4. [13-14th c.]

ROCKE

ROBINSON, C. J. 'Rocke family', N.Q.S.D., 3, 1893, p.164-5.

RODNEY

RODNEY, Sir Edward. 'The genealogy of the family of Rodney of Rodney Stoke', Genealogist, N.S., 16, 1900, p.207-14; 17, 1901, p.6-12 & 100-106.

ROGERS

ROGERS, W. H. Hamilton. 'Rogers-Courtenay-Huddesfield, of Bradford-on-Avon, Wilts., Cannington, Somerset, and Shillingford, Dorset', in his Archaeological papers relating to the counties of Somerset, Wilts, Hants and Devon. [ ]: the author, 1902.

R., W. H. H. 'Rogers of Brianston, Dorset, and Barwick, Somerset', N.Q.S.D., 8, 1903, p.290-4 & 337-42. See also 9, 1905, p.61.

'The Lady Mary Harington's pedigree (nee Rogers of Cannington, Somerset)', M.G.H., N.S., 3, 1880, p.219-20.

See also Harington

ROSEWELL

LONGDEN, H. I. 'Rosewell family', N.Q.S.D., 3, 1893, p.185. [Includes will of William Rosewell of Dunkerton, 1565-6]

ROSSE

DENARIUS. 'Rosse of Shepton Beauchamp, Co. Somerset', Genealogist, N.S., 17, 1901, p.72. [Pedigree, 18th c.]

RUSS

CURNOW, E. 'Russ of Kingsbury', G.T., 12(3), 1987, p.86. [New Zealand migrants]

LINDSAY, Kay L. 'Russ of Tintinhull, Martock and Stoke Sub Hamden', G.T., 9(2), 1984, p.54-6. [Includes pedigree, 17-20th c.]

RUSSELL

See Rawlins

ST. CLAIR

WILLIAMS, C. L. Sinclair. 'The manor of Stapleton in Martock and the St. Clairs', S.A.N.H.S., 131, 1986/7, p.171-80. [11-14th c.]

SAMBORNE

SANBORNE, V. S. 'A possible Samborne ancestry', Ancestor, 1, 1904, p.61-70. [Somerset, Wiltshire, & Berkshire]

'Pedigree of Samborne, from visitation of London, 1687', Genealogist, 1, 1877, p.218-9. [Of Somerset & London; 16-18th c.]

SEABOROUGH

See Golde

SEAMAN

JEBOULT, Edward. An epitome of the history of the Seaman family of Shiplette manor, Somerset. Taunton: the author, 1891. [Also includes information on Hippisley family]

See also Hippisley

SEWARD

SQUIBB, G. D. 'Seward family of Yeovil', N.Q.S.D., 25, 1950, p.234-7. [17th c.]

SEYMOUR

LOCKE, A. Audrey. The Seymour family: history and romance. London: Constable, 1911.

ST. MAUR, H. Annals of the Seymours, being a history of the Seymour family from early times to within a few years of the present. London: Kegan Paul, Trench, Trubner & Co., 1902. [Devon & Somerset]

SHARPE

SCHOMBERG, A. 'Sharpe family', N.Q.S.D., 3, 1893, p.105-7. [Memoranda book giving dates of birth]

SHEATE

'Connections', G.T., 10(3), 1985, p.107. [List of families connected with Sheate of Baltonsborough and New Zealand, 18-20th c.]

SHEPPARD

GILL, D. J. The Sheppards and eighteenth century Frome. Frome : Frome Society for Local Study, 1982.

SHUMACK

SHUMACK, John. The Shumack family. Wisbech: Ye Olde Prynt Shoppe, 1982.

SHUTE

HYLTON, Lord. 'Kilmersdon manor-house', S.A.N.H.S., 75, 1929, p.42-5. [Shute family; 17-19th c.]

SIDERFIN

SANDERS, James. History of the Siderfin family of West Somerset. Exeter: W. J. Southwood & Co., 1912.

SKRINE

WALKER, E. W. Ainley. Skrine of Warleigh in the county of Somerset, with pedigrees, being some materials for a genealogical history of the family of Skrine. Taunton: Wessex Press, 1936.

SKUTT

NIGHTINGALE, J. E. 'Grant of arms to John Skutt', N.Q.S.D., 1, 1890, p.232-4. [Includes genealogical notes]

POYNTON, F. J. 'Skutt notes', N.Q.S.D., 2, 1891, p.17-18. [Includes 16th c. pedigree]

SMITH

BRYANT, Edith. 'Smith of Devon and Somerset - Smith of Cornwall', Devon & Cornwall notes & queries., 16, 1930-31, p.250-3.

See also Montagu

SMITH-WYNDHAM

See Rawlins

SMYTH

BANTOCK, Anton. The earlier Smyths of Ashton Court from their letters, 1545-1741. Bristol: Malago Society, 1982. [Includes pedigree]

BANTOCK, Anton. The inside story of the Smyths of Ashton Court. Bristol: Malago Archives Committee, 1977.

BANTOCK, A. The later Smyths of Ashton Court: from their letters, 1741-1802. Bristol: Malago Society, 1984.

BETTEY, J. H. Calendar of the correspondence of the Smyth family of Ashton Court, 1548-1642. Bristol Record Society, 35. Bristol: the Society, 1982.

BETTEY, J. H. The rise of a gentry family: the Smyths of Ashton Court, c.1500-1642. Bristol: Historical Association, 1978.

WAY, Lewis Upton. 'The Smyths of Ashton Court', Transactions of the Bristol & Gloucestershire Archaeological Society, 31, 1908, p.244-60.

SMYTHIES

'Pedigree of the Smythies family', M.G.H, 4th series, 4, 1912, p.170-82, 193-200, 276-86, 306-19, & 354-63.

SNIGG

JEWERS, A. J. 'Snigg family', N.Q.S.D., 5, 1897-8, p.276-7. [17-18th c.]

SPEKE

MURDOCH, Sophia. Record of the Speke family (Jordans, Somerset). Reading: H. T. Morley, [1900]. [Of Somerset, Devon, Yorkshire, Lancashire, Wiltshire and Berkshire]

PINE-COFFIN, Matilda. The Speke family. Exeter: Godfrey & Bartlett, 1914.

SNELL, F. J. 'A family of politicians', in his Memorials of old Somerset. London: Bemrose & Sons, 1906, p.218-38. [Speke family, 17-18th c.]

STAWELL

STAWELL, George Dodsworth, ed. A Quantock family: the Stawells of Cothelstone and their descendants, the barons Stawell of Somerton, and the Stawells of Devonshire and the county Cork. Taunton: Barnicott & Pearce, Wessex Press, 1910.

STAYNINGS

WILLIAMS, M. 'Staynings family', M.G.H., N.S., 3, 1880, p.20-2. [Includes the will of Charles Staynings of Holnycote, Somerset, 1693]

STEPHENS

See Clarke

STOATE

STOATE, Thomas L., & STOATE, Geoffrey L. Records of the Stoate family. Bristol: Stonebridge Press, 1965. [17-19th c.]

STOCKER

See Sydenham

STONE

COOKE, Robert. 'Stone of Wedmore: a lost gentry family?', G.T., 4(2), 1979, p.15-16.

MEAD, L. G. 'Stones of Wiveliscombe', G.T., 13(1), 1988, p.11.

STOURTON

WERE, F. 'Stourton pedigree', N.Q.S.D., 9, 1905, p.125-9.

STRANGWAYS

'Not so strange', G.T., 13(2), 1988, p.46.

STRECHLEIGH

See Golde

STRODE

BATEN, John. 'Additional note on Barrington and the Strodes', S.A.N.H.S., 37(2), 1891, p.40-43.

BROWN, Fredk. 'Pedigrees of the Strode family', S.A.N.H.S., 30(2), 1884, p.66-73. [16-18th c.]

DYER, A. S. 'Strode of Somerset', Notes & queries, 187, 1944, p.80 & 166-7; 188, 1945, p.19-20. [16-18th c.]

SEREL, T. 'On the Strodes of Somerset', S.A.N.H.S., 13(2), 1865-6, p.6-20.

STRONG

'Strong family of Somerset', N.Q.S.D., 2, 1891, p.51-2.

STUCKEY

CHURCHMAN, Michael. The Starkeys of Somerset. Englewood, Colorado: the author, c.1966.

STURGE

See Clarke

SWINNERTON

MARTIN, E. H. 'Swinnerton-Dyer family', N.Q.S.D., 10, 1907, p.309-27 & 341-52; 11, 1909, p.24-35. See also 11, 1909, p.75-7. [17-19th c.]

SYDENHAM

HEAD, H. S. 'Sydenham of Brympton', M.G.H., 2nd series, 3, 1890, p.323-36. & 349-51. [Includes pedigree]

JEWERS, Arthur J. 'Sydenham pedigree', N.Q.S.D., 8, 1903, p.315-21. See also 9, 1905, p.38.

MARSHALL, J. C. 'Sydenham heraldry', N.Q.S.D., 16, 1920, p.19-23.

SYDENHAM, G. F. The history of the Sydenham family, collected from family documents, pedigrees, deeds, and copious memoranda, edited by A. T. Cameron. East Molesey, Surrey: E. Dwelly, 1928. [Includes monumental inscriptions, extensive list of wills, many pedigrees, etc., etc]

STOCKER, Charles J. S. 'Sydenham and Stocker families', N.Q.S.D., 18, 1926, p.25-6. See also 17, 1923, p.290.

SYMCOKE

POYNTON, F. J. 'Symcoke and Jessop', N.Q.S.D., 3, 1893, p.152-3. [Stray from Butleigh, marrying at Worksop, Nottinghamshire]

SYMONDS

SYMONDS, H. A memoir of the family of Symonds in Somerset and Dorset, with some account of their connexions by marriage. Taunton: Wessex Press, 1933.

TASSELL

'Tassell family', N.Q.S.D., 28, 1968, p.218-9. [17-18th c.]

THORNER

See Harington

TITFORD

TITFORD, J. The Titford story: come wind, come weather. Chichester: Phillimore, 1988. See also G.T., 13(1), 1988, p.16-17.

TREAT

TREAT, John Harvey. The Treat family: a genealogy of Trott, Tratt and Treat for fifteen generations, and four hundred and fifty years, in England and America. Salem, Mass: Salem Press, 1893.

TREVELYAN

BUSH, R. J. E. 'Nettlecombe Court, 1: the Trevelyans and other residents at the Court', Field studies, 32, 1970, p.275-87. [Includes pedigree showing descent of Nettlecombe through Ralegh, Whalesburgh, Trevelyan and Wolseley, 12-20th c.]

TUSON

COX, J. S. The Tuson family of Ilchester. St. Peter Port: Toucan, 1984.

URTIACO

BATES, E. H. 'The family of De Urtiaco', S.A.N.H.S., 42(2), 1896, p.26-55. [Medieval]

VAGG

VAGG, C. Mervyn. Somerset Vaggs in Australia: a short history of the Somerset family of Vagg, and their pioneers in early Australia. Elwood: Vagg Family Reunion Committee, 1960.

VALLETORT

BENSON, J. 'Valletort of Somerset', Devon & Cornwall notes & queries, 20(8), 1939, p.355-61.

VENNER

VENNER, D. The Venners of Somerset and Devon. South Molton: the author, 1980.

VOWELL

HOLLOWAY, Estelle. Elinor with the leading eyes. Williton: Williton Printers, [198-?] [Vowell family; Devon, Somerset & Norfolk]

'Prior Vowell and his Kinsmen', N.Q.S.D., 18, 1926, p.10-11. [Includes pedigrees 15-16th c.]

WADHAM

D., W. 'Wadham family', N.Q.S.D., 1, 1890, p.101-2.

PESKETT, H. M. 'The Wadham family estates', Devon and Cornwall notes and queries, 31, 1968-70, p.238-45. See also 32, 1971-3, p.93-4. [14-18th c; of Wadham and Seaton, Devon, and Merifield, Somerset]

WYNDHAM, William. 'The Wadhams and Merifield', S.A.N.H.S., 80(2), 1934, p.1-10.

WALKER

'Dalison notes: Walker pedigree from visitation of Somerset, 1623', M.G.H., 2nd series, 1888, p.241. [Walker & Dalison families]

WANSTROW

See Harding

WARRE

GIBSON, William. 'A continuous patrimony: the Warres of Hestercombe & Cheddon Fitzpaine', S.A.N.H.S., 132, 1987/8, p.181-2. [14-19th c.]

WEEKES

WEEKES, Robt. D. Genealogy of the family of George Weekes of Dorchester, Mass, part II. Newark, New Jersey: the author, 1892. [Devon and Somerset]

WELLESLEY

SEREL, T. 'The origin of the names of Wellesley and the early connection of the family with Wells', S.A.N.H.S., 12(2), 1863-4, p.177-89. [Medieval]

WERE

FOX, J. H. The woollen manufacturers at Wellington, Somerset, compiled from the records of an old family business. London: A. L. Humphreys, 1914. [Includes pedigrees of Were and Fox families, 17-19th c.]

WESCOMBE

'Pedigree of Wescombe of Fiddington, Co. Somerset', M.G.H., 5th series, 1, 1916, p.276.

DODDERIDGE, S. E. 'Wescombe of Doddington, Co. Somerset', M.G.H., 5th series, 1, 1916, p.155-7.

DODDERIDGE, Sidney E. 'Westcombe, alias Wescombe, Cos. Somerset and Devon', N.Q.S.D., 10, 1907, p.252-9. See also 11, 1909, p.329-32. [16-19th c.]

WHALESBURGH

See Trevelyan

WHITE

See Harington

WHITMORE

WHITE, Elizabeth. 'The Whitmores and the manor of Keynsham', S.A.N.H.S., 129, 1984/5, p.155-60. [17-18th c.]

WILLIS

CHURCH, E. M. 'Willis-Drury', N.Q.S.D., 3, 1893, p.101. See also p.133, 176-8, & 220-1.

WITHIPOLL

DUNLOP, J. R. 'Pedigree of the Withipoll family of Somersetshire, Shropshire, Essex, and Suffolk', M.G.H., 5th series, 5, 1923-25, p.378-86.

WOLSELEY

See Trevelyan

WOOD

FALCONER, J. P. E. 'Family of John Wood of Bath', Notes & queries, 193, 1948, p.403-8. [Includes pedigree, 18th c., monumental inscriptions, and will of John Wood of Walcot, 1753]

ROBINSON, C. J. 'Dr. Gerard Wood, Archdeacon of Wells', N.Q.S.D., 3, 1893, p.341. [Genealogical information from the civil war proceedings of the Committee for Compounding with Delinquents]

WYATT

BLOOM, J. H. 'Wyatt family', M.G.H., 6th series, 8, 1932-4, p.49-53. [Includes extracts from the parish register and manor court rolls of Priston, Somerset, together with wills]

WYNDHAM

WYNDHAM, Ailward. 'Kentsford, Watchet and the Wyndham family', N.Q.S.D., 23, 1942, p.299-305.

WYNDHAM, H. A. A family history, 1410-1688: the Wyndhams of Norfolk and Somerset. London: Oxford University Press, 1939.

WYNDHAM, H. A. A family history 1688-1837: the Wyndhams of Somerset, Sussex and Wiltshire. London: Oxford University Press, 1950.

See also Rawlins

YEA

MONDAY, Alfred James. The history of the family of Yea ... Taunton: G. Vincent, 1885. [Somerset, Devon & Dorset]

YEOMAN

See Harding

YESCOMBE

'The Yescombe family: Yescombes of Blackford', G.T., 8(2), p.54-5. [16-18th c]

CHAPTER 8
PARISH REGISTERS AND OTHER RECORDS OF BIRTHS, MARRIAGES, AND DEATHS

Registers of births, marriages and deaths are normally one of the first sources to be consulted by genealogists. For Somerset, they are listed in:

MEDLYCOTT, Mervyn T. 'Parish registers at the County Record Offices', G.T., 1(2), 1976, p.22; 1(3), 1970, p.36; 2(2), 1977, p.21; 3(2), 1978, p.25; 4(2), 1979, p.12; 5(2), p.11; 6(2), 1981, p.36; 7(2), 1982, p.39; 8(2), 1983, p.42; 9(2), 1984, p.39; 10(3), 1985, p.115; 10(4), 1985, p.148.

A number of early bishops' transcripts of registers are printed in:

JEWERS, Arthur J., ed. The first portion of the bishops'transcripts at Wells, being those that are in the most fragile condition. Dwelly's parish records, vols. 1-2. Herne Bay: E. Dwelly, 1913-1914. [Section 1: parishes A-H; section 2: parishes H-Y. A supplement is printed in Dwelly's parish records, 15, 1926.]

Further brief extracts from bishops' transcripts, relating to families who entered their pedigrees at heraldic visitations, are printed in:

JEWERS, A. J. 'Parish register notes (Somerset)', N.Q.S.D., 12, 1911, p.158-63.

Pre 1558 registers are listed in:

SAUNDERS, G. W. 'Early parochial registers in the Diocese of Bath and Wells, N.Q.S.D., 23, 1942, p.172-5.

The British Library holds a number of parish register transcripts. Some are listed in:

FURLONG, Nancy G. 'Registers of parishes in the Deaneries of Bath and Keynsham', G.T., 5(2), 1980, p.14-15.

Extracts from parish registers of South-East Somerset are given in:

'Bennett mss', N.Q.S.D., 28, 1968, p.177-8, 202-4, 225-6, 247-8, 270-1, 292-3.

For a brief and rather dated discussion of Somerset registers, see:

BAKER, Ernest R. 'Notes from Somerset parish registers', Western antiquary, 6(10), 1887, p.235-7 & 262-4.

For mid-seventeenth century marriages, see:

JEWERS, A. J. 'Commonwealth marriages, Somerset', 1653-6', N.Q.S.D., 2, 1891, p.73-80 & 104-11.

Nonconformist registers are listed in:

DWELLY, Edward. 'Somerset non-parochial registers', S.A.N.H.S., 79(2), 1933, p.31-8. See also: HANSFORD, Michael A. 'Somerset non-parochial registers', G.T., 6(2), 1981, p.39-42.

For marriage licences, see:

JEWERS, Arthur J. Marriage allegation bonds of the bishops of Bath and Wells from their commencement to the year 1755. 2 vols. Exeter: W. Pollard & Co., 1909. Supplement to Genealogist, N.S., 15-26.

For licences, 1606-33, where one party was not a Somersetian, see:

'Wells marriage licences', N.Q.S.D., 23, 1942, p.39-40, 65-8, & 73-5.

Many Somersetians obtained their marriage licences in Bristol. See:

RALPH, Elizabeth, ed. Marriage bonds for the diocese of Bristol, excluding the Archdeaconry of Dorset. Vol. 1: 1637-1700. Bristol & Gloucestershire Archaeological Society Records Section, 1. Bristol: the Society, 1954.

For Ilminster licences, 1709-34, see:

BATTEN, John. 'The royal peculiar of Ilminster', N.Q.S.D., 7, 1901, p.13-17.

Many Somersetians married in other counties. A number of lists of Somerset 'strays' have been published:

BAKER, T. H. 'Marriages of Somerset and Dorset people celebrated in other counties', N.Q.S.D., 7, 1901, p.315-6. [From Kingston Deverill and Monkton Deverill, Wiltshire, parish registers]

H., J. J. 'Somerset and Dorset marriages at Boyton, Wilts', N.Q.S.D., 57-8.

BAKER, Thomas H. 'Somerset and Dorset marriages', N.Q.S.D., 12, 1911, p.165-6. [At Stratford-sub-Castle, Fisherton Anger, West Harnham, Idmiston, and Laverstock, Wiltshire]

S[KINNER], A. J. P. 'Somerset entries in the parish registers of Seaton, Devon', N.Q.S.D., 14, 1915, p.35.

Many individual parish registers have been published; these are listed below. Also listed here are a number of brief descriptions of registers, some of which include extracts. The Phillimore parish register series (P.P.R.S.) included many Somerset registers: a ms. index to these is described in:

ABORIGINAL. 'The Dwelly index', G.T., 13(1), 1988, p.25. [This also notes an index to Colonial Office documents relating to Australia, 1787-96.]

ABBAS COMBE

DWELLY, E., & T. W., eds. Bishops' transcripts at Wells, vol. 3, being all the unpublished transcripts for the parishes A-Ashill. Herne Bay: E. Dwelly, 1915.

AISHOLT

'Marriages at Aisholt, 1654 to 1811', in PHILLIMORE, W. P. W., BELL, W. A., & WHISTLER, C. W., eds. Somerset parish registers: marriages, 6. P.P.R.S., 54. London: Phillimore, 1905, p.1-7.

See also Abbas Combe

ALFORD

See Abbas Combe

ALLER

'Marriages at Aller, 1560 to 1812', in PHILLIMORE, W. P. W., & HAYWARD, Douglas L, eds. Somerset parish registers: marriages, 1. P.P.R.S., 5. London: Phillimore, 1898, p.1-21.

See Abbas Combe

ALLERTON

See Abbas Combe

ALMSFORD

See Abbas Combe

ANGERSLEIGH

EASTWOOD, Arthur, ed. 'Marriages at Angersleigh, 1693 to 1812', in PHILLIMORE, W. P. W., & SEAGER, H. W., eds. Somerset parish registers: marriages, 7. P.P.R.S., 69. London: Phillimore, 1905, p.1-5.

See also Abbas Combe

ANSFORD

See Ash Priors

ASHBRITTLE

SEAGER, H. W., ed. 'Marriages at Ashbrittle, 1563 to 1812', in PHILLIMORE, W. P. W., & SEAGER, H. W., eds. Somerset parish registers: marriages, 11. P.P.R.S., 114. London: Phillimore, 1906, p.107-23.

See also Abbas Combe

ASHCOTT

See Abbas Combe

ASHILL

POOLE, R. B., ed. 'Marriages at Ashill, 1558 to 1815', in PHILLIMORE, W. P. W., & BATES, E. H., eds. Somerset parish registers: marriages, 4. P.P.R.S., 30. London: Phillimore, 1902, p.1-17.

See Abbas Combe

ASHINGTON

See Ash Priors

ASH PRIORS

DWELLY, E., ed. Bishops' transcripts at Wells, vol.4: being all the unpublished transcripts for the parishes Ash Priors, Ashington, Ashwick, Axbridge, Babcary, Babington, Backwell, Badgworth, South Barrow, also Ansford, 1807 and Wrington, 1806-7. Dwelly's parish records, 5. Fleet, Hants: E. Dwelly, 1917.

SEAGER, H. W., ed. 'Marriages at Ash Priors, 1700 to 1812', in PHILLIMORE, W. P. W., & SEAGER, H. W., eds. Somerset parish registers: marriages, 8. P.P.R.S., 68. London: Phillimore, 1906, p.79-83.

ASHWICK

See Ash Priors

AXBRIDGE

See Ash Priors

BABCARY

See Ash Priors

BABINGTON

See Ash Priors

BACKWELL

See Ash Priors

BADGWORTH

See Ash Priors

BARRINGTON

HAMLET, J., et al, eds. 'Marriages at Barrington, 1654 to 1812', in PHILLIMORE, W. P. W., & BATES, E. H., eds. Somerset parish registers: marriages, 4. P.P.R.S., 30. London: Phillimore, 1902, p.75-83.

BARROW GURNEY

WERE, F., ed. 'Marriages at Barrow Gurney, 1593 to 1812', in PHILLIMORE, W. P. W., & HAYWARD, Douglas L, eds. Somerset parish registers: marriages, 2. P.P.R.S., 7. London: Phillimore, 1899, p.141-53.

BARWICK

BATES HARBIN, E. H. 'Notes on the registers of Barwick near Yeovil', N.Q.S.D., 15, 1917, p.74-9.

BATH

JEWERS, A. J., ed. The registers of the Abbey Church of Ss. Peter and Paul, Bath. Harleian Society registers, 27-8. London: the Society, 1900-1.

DWELLY, E., & T. W., eds. Bishops' transcripts at Wells, vol. 5: being all the unpublished transcripts for Bath to 1793-4 and Othery 1608. Dwelly's parish records, 7. Fleet: E. Dwelly, 1919.

DWELLY, E., ed. Bishops' transcripts at Wells, vol. 6: Bath, 1768-1802, Durston, Chipstable, Raddington, Northover, Ilchester, and Broadway, 1598-1628. Dwelly's parish records, 9. Fleet, Hants: E. Dwelly, 1922.

STROTHER, A. 'Extracts from the burial register of St. James, Bath', Genealogist, N.S., 8, 1982, p.186-7 & 251-2; N.S., 9, 1893, p.36-40 & 109-12.

STROTHER, A. 'Extracts of burials from the registers of Bath Abbey', Genealogist, N.S., 6, 1890, p.92-101 & 183-7.

STROTHER, A. 'Extracts from the burial register of St. Michael's Bath', Genealogist, N.S., 10, 1894, p.105-9. [1569-1839]

BEER CROCOMBE

POOLE, R. B., ed. 'Marriages at Beer Crocombe, 1542 to 1812', in PHILLIMORE, W. P. W., & BATES, D. H., eds., Somerset parish registers: marriages, 4. P.P.R.S., 30. London: Phillimore, 1901, p.25-33.

BICKENHALL

See Staple Fitzpaine

BISHOPS' HULL

SEAGER, H. W., ed. 'Marriages at Bishops' Hull, 1562 to 1812', in PHILLIMORE, W. P. W., SEAGER, H. W., & BATES, E. H., eds. Somerset parish registers: marriages, 10. P.P.R.S., 88. London: Phillimore, 1906, p.115-42.

BRADFORD

SEAGER, H. W., ed. 'Marriages at Bradford, 1558 to 1812', in PHILLIMORE, W. P. W., & SEAGER, H. W., eds. Somerset parish registers: marriages, 7. P.P.R.S., 69. London: Phillimore, 1905, p.125-54.

BROADWAY

See Bath

BROOMFIELD

'Marriages at Broomfield, 1630 to 1812', in PHILLIMORE, W. P. W., BELL, W. A., & WHISTLER, C. W., eds. Somerset parish registers: marriages, 6. P.P.R.S., 54. London: Phillimore, 1905, p.9-22.

BRUTON

HAYWARD, Douglas L., ed. The registers of Bruton, Co. Somerset ... 2 vols. London: Parish Register Society, 1907-11. [v.1: 1554-1680; v.2: 1681-1812]

W[EAVER], F. W. 'Bruton registers', N.Q.S.D., 6, 1899, p.115-6. [Note]

BUCKLAND ST. MARY

LANCE, W. H., ed. 'Marriages at Buckland St. Mary, 1538 to 1812', in PHILLIMORE, W. P. W., & BATES, E. H., eds. Somerset parish registers: marriages, 4. P.P.R.S., 30. London: Phillimore, 1902, p.107-24.

BURNHAM

COLEMAN, J. Notes from Burnham, Somerset', N.Q.S.D., 3, 1893, p.265-7. [Includes many death notices, early 19th c.]

BUTCOMBE

BRITTEN, Ethel Elizabeth, & HOLMYARD, Eric John. Marriages at Butcombe, Somersetshire, 1605-1835. London: De La More Press, 1913.

CANNINGTON

BELL, W. A. , ed. 'Marriages at Cannington, 1559 to 1812', in PHILLIMORE, W. P. W., BELL, W. A., & WHISTLER, C. W., eds. Somerset parish registers: marriages, 6. P.P.R.S., 54. London: Phillimore, 1905, p.89-128.

CHARLTON ADAM

BRYAN, Mrs. 'Marriages at Charlton Adam, 1707 to 1812', in PHILLIMORE, W. P. W., & HAYWARD, Douglas L, eds. Somerset parish registers: marriages, 1. P.P.R.S., 5. London: Phillimore, 1898, p.23-8.

CHARLTON MACKRELL

'Marriages at Charlton Mackrell, 1575 to 1812', in PHILLIMORE, W. P. W., & HAYWARD, Douglas L, eds. Somerset parish registers: marriages, 1. P.P.R.S., 5. London: Phillimore, 1898, p.29-47.

CHARLYNCH

'Marriages at Charlynch, 1745 to 1779', in PHILLIMORE, W. P. W., BELL, W. A., & WHISTLER, C. W., eds. Somerset parish registers: marriages, 6. P.P.R.S., 54. London: Phillimore, 1905, p.23-4.

CHEDDAR

COLEMAN, J. 'A lost Cheddar register', N.Q.S.D., 3, 1893, p.38. [Discussion of a missing register]

CHEDDON FITZPAINE

SEAGER, H. W., ed. 'Marriages at Cheddon Fitzpaine, 1559 to 1812', in PHILLIMORE, W. P. W., & SEAGER, H. W., eds. Somerset parish registers: marriages, 8. P.P.R.S., 68. London: Phillimore, 1906, p.105-20.

CHEDZOY

BELL, W. A., ed. 'Marriages at Chedzoy, 1558 to 1812', in PHILLIMORE, W. P. W., & BELL, W. A., eds. Somerset parish registers: marriages, 12. P.P.R.S., 122. London: Phillimore, 1910, p.99-121.

CHIPSTABLE

DWELLY, E., ed. (Somerset) parish registers, vol. 1, of Chipstable, Raddington, Kittisford, and Pitcombe. Dwelly's parish records, 8. Topsham: E. Dwelly, 1921. [Also includes monumental inscriptions and list of Chipstable rectors]

See also Bath

COMBE ST. NICHOLAS

'Combe St. Nicholas', N.Q.S.D., 22, 1937, p.124-7. [Extracts from Combe St. Nicholas & Winsham parish registers, 1678-97]

CHADWICK, J. M., ed. 'Marriages at Combe St. Nicholas, 1678 to 1812', in BLAGG, Thos. M., & PHILLIMORE, W. P. W., eds. Somerset parish registers: marriages, 14. P.P.R.S., 170. London: Phillimore, 1913, p.1-23.

CORFE

SEAGER, H. W. ed. 'Marriages at Corfe, 1687 to 1812', in PHILLIMORE, W. P. W., & SEAGER, H. W., eds. Somerset parish registers: marriages, 7. P.P.R.S., 69. London: Phillimore, 1905, p.65-7.

COTHELSTONE

SEAGER, H. W., ed. 'Marriages at Cothelstone,, 1664 to 1715', in PHILLIMORE, W. P. W., & SEAGER, H. W., eds. Somerset parish registers: marriages, 8. P.P.R.S., 68. London: Phillimore, 1906, p.75-8.

CREECH ST. MICHAEL

SEAGER, H.W., ed. 'Marriages at Creech St. Michael, 1665 to 1814', in PHILLIMORE, W. P. W., & SEAGER, H. W., eds. Somerset parish registers: marriages, 7. P.P.R.S., 69. London: Phillimore, 1905, p.107-24.

CREWKERNE

ROSS, D. M., ed. 'Marriages at Crewkerne, 1559 to 1812', in PHILLIMORE, W. P. W., & ROSS, D. M., eds. Somerset parish registers: marriages, 5. P.P.R.S., 49. London: Phillimore, 1904, p.1-111.

BARRETT, John. 'Marriages from the parish registers of Crewkerne, 1559 to 1812', G.T., 7(1), 1981, p.11-13. [Statistical discussion]

CRICKET ST. THOMAS

BATES HARBIN, E. H. 'Cricket St. Thomas register, 1564-1768', N.Q.S.D., 15, 1917, p.172-6.

CROWCOMBE

BELL, W. A., ed. 'Marriages at Crowcombe, 1641 to 1812', in PHILLIMORE, W. P. W., & BELL, W. A., eds. Somerset parish registers: marriages, 12. P.P.R.S., 122. London: Phillimore, 1910, p.133-47.

CURRY RIVEL

'Marriages at Curry Rivel, 1642 to 1812', in PHILLIMORE, W. P. W., & ROSS, D. M., eds., Somerset parish registers: marriages, 3. P.P.R.S., 23. London: Phillimore, 1901, p.121-54.

DODINGTON

BELL, W. A., ed. 'Marriages at Dodington, 1538 to 1805', in PHILLIMORE, W. P. W., BELL, W. A., & WHISTLER, C. W., eds. Somerset parish registers: marriages, 6. P.P.R.S., 54. London: Phillimore, 1905, p.25-31.

DRAYTON

'Marriages at Drayton, 1577 to 1812', in PHILLIMORE, W. P. W., & ROSS, D. M., eds., Somerset parish registers: marriages, 3. P.P.R.S., 23. London: Phillimore, 1901, p.101-19.

DURLEIGH

BELL, W. A., ed. 'Marriages at Durleigh, 1683 to 1807', in PHILLIMORE, W. P. W., BELL, W. A., & WHISTLER, C. W., eds. Somerset parish registers: marriages, 6. P.P.R.S., 54. London: Phillimore, 1905, p.33-9.

DURSTON

BARTLETT, R. Grosvenor, ed. The registers of Durston, Co. Somerset, 1712-1812. Parish Register Society, 71. London: the Society, 1914.

See also Bath

EAST PENNARD

DANIEL, W. E. 'East Pennard registers', N.Q.S.D., 3, 1893, p.211-3. [Includes a few selected entries, 1617-1746]

BARTELOT, T. Grosvenor, ed. 'Marriages at East Pennard, 1608 to 1817', in BLAGG, Thos. M., & PHILLIMORE, W. P. W., eds. Somerset parish registers: marriages, 14. P.P.R.S., 170. London: Phillimore, 1913, p.85-104.

EAST QUANTOXHEAD

BELL, W. A., ed. 'Marriages at East Quantoxhead, 1654 to 1812', in PHILLIMORE, W. P. W., & BELL, W. A., eds. Somerset parish registers: marriages, 12. P.P.R.S., 122. London: Phillimore, 1910, p.61-7.

DODDERIDGE, Sidney E. 'East Quantoxhead marriages', N.Q.S.D., 19, 1929, p.65. [Bishops' transcripts of marriages, 1598-1640, not in Phillimore]

ENMORE

BELL, W. A., ed. 'Marriages at Enmore, 1653 to 1812', in PHILLIMORE, W. P. W., BELL, W. A., & WHISTLER, C. W., eds. Somerset parish registers: marriages, 6. P.P.R.S., 54. London: Phillimore, 1905, p.41-50.

FIDDINGTON

BELL, W. A., ed. 'Marriages at Fiddington, 1706 to 1812', in PHILLIMORE, W. P. W., & BELL, W. A., eds. Somerset parish registers: marriages, 12. P.P.R.S., 122. London: Phillimore, 1910, p.69-72.

FIVEHEAD

'Marriages at Fivehead, 1656 to 1812', in PHILLIMORE, W. P. W., & ROSS, D. M., eds. Somerset parish registers: marriages, 5. P.P.R.S., 49. London: Phillimore, 1904, p.117-22.

GOATHURST

BELL, W. A., ed. 'Marriages at Goathurst, 1539 to 1812', in PHILLIMORE, W. P. W., & BELL, W. A., eds. Somerset parish registers: marriages, 12. P.P.R.S., 122. London: Phillimore, 1910, p.83-98.

BROWN, F., ed. 'Extracts from the parish registers of Goathurst, Somerset', Genealogist, N.S., 2, 1885, p.50-2 & 96-7.

HALSE

'Marriages at Halse, 1559 to 1812', in PHILLIMORE, W. P. W., SEAGER, H. W., & BATES, E. H., eds. Somerset parish registers: marriages, 10. P.P.R.S., 88. London: Phillimore, 1906, p.143-58.

HEATHFIELD

SEAGER, H. W., ed. 'Marriages at Heathfield, 1700 to 1812', in PHILLIMORE, W. P. W., & SEAGER, H. W., eds. Somerset parish registers: marriages, 8. P.P.R.S., 68. London: Phillimore, 1906, p.13-18.

HIGH HAM

CROSSMAN, C. D., ed. 'Marriages at High Ham, 1569 to 1812', in PHILLIMORE, W. P. W., & HAYWARD, Douglas L, eds. Somerset parish registers: marriages, 1. P.P.R.S., 5. London: Phillimore, 1898, p.49-80.

HILL FARRANCE

SEAGER, H. W. ed. 'Marriages at Hill Farrance, 1701 to 1812', in PHILLIMORE, W. P. W., & SEAGER, H. W., eds. Somerset parish registers: marriages, 8. P.P.R.S., 68. London: Phillimore, 1906, p.1-12.

HINTON ST. GEORGE

LOWE, D., ed. 'Marriages at Hinton St. George, 1632 to 1837', in PHILLIMORE, W. P. W., & SEAGER, H. W., eds. Somerset parish registers: marriages, 13. P.P.R.S., 131. London: Phillimore, 1910, p.29-48.

HOLFORD

BELL, W. A., ed. 'Marriages at Holford, 1558 to 1812', in PHILLIMORE, W. P. W., & BELL, W. A., eds. Somerset parish registers: marriages, 12. P.P.R.S., 122. London: Phillimore, 1910. p.73-82.

HORSINGTON

DANIEL, W. E. The parish register of Horsington, in the county of Somerset, 1558-1836. Frome Selwood: Broadway Press, 1907.

HUISH EPISCOPI

'Marriages at Huish Episcopi, 1698 to 1812', in PHILLIMORE, W. P. W., & HAYWARD, Douglas L, eds. Somerset parish registers: marriages, 1. P.P.R.S., 5. London: Phillimore, 1898, p.81-9.

ILCHESTER

See Bath

ISLE ABBOTS

GIBBON, H., ed. 'Marriages at Ile-Abbots, 1562 to 1837', in BLAGG, Thos. M., & PHILLIMORE, W. P. W., eds. Somerset parish registers: marriages, 14. P.P.R.S., 170. London: Phillimore, 1913, p.47-60.

ISLE BREWER

COLES, A. B., ed. 'Marriages at Ile Brewers, 1705 to 1812', in PHILLIMORE, W. P. W., & BATES, E. H., eds., Somerset parish registers: marriages, 4. P.P.R.S., 30. London: Phillimore, 1901, p.19-24.

ILMINSTER

DUKE, J., ed. 'Marriages at Ilminster, 1662 to 1812', in PHILLIMORE, W. P. W., & SEAGER, H. W., eds. Somerset parish registers: marriages, 13. P.P.R.S., 131. London: Phillimore, 1910, p.49-89.

ILTON

POOLE, R. B., ed. 'Marriages at Ilton, 1642 to 1811', in PHILLIMORE, W. P. W., & BATES, E. H., eds., Somerset parish registers: marriages, 4. P.P.R.S., 30. London: Phillimore, 1901., p.35-50.

KILMINGTON

LLOYD, John A., ed. 'Marriages at Kilmington, 1705 to 1837', in BLAGG, Thos. M., & PHILLIMORE, W. P. W., eds. Somerset parish registers: marriages, 14. P.P.R.S., 170. London: Phillimore, 1913, p.65-83. [Actually 1582-1837]

KILTON

BELL, W. A., ed. 'Marriages at Kilton, 1683 to 1812', in PHILLIMORE, W. P. W., & BELL, W. A., eds. Somerset parish registers: marriages, 12. P.P.R.S., 122. London: Phillimore, 1910, p.161-5.

KILVE

BELL, W. A., ed. 'Marriages at Kilve, 1638 to 1812', in PHILLIMORE, W. P. W., & BELL, W. A., eds. Somerset parish registers: marriages, 12. P.P.R.S., 122. London: Phillimore, 1910, p.123-31.

KINGSBURY EPISCOPI

ROSS, D. M., ed. 'Marriages at Kingsbury Episcopi,1557 to 1812', in PHILLIMORE, W. P. W., & ROSS, D. M., eds. Somerset parish registers: marriages, 5. P.P.R.S., 49. London: Phillimore, 1904, p.123-64.

KINGSDON

'Marriages at Kingsdon, 1540 to 1812', in PHILLIMORE, W. P. W., & HAYWARD, Douglas L, eds. Somerset parish registers: marriages, 1. P.P.R.S., 5. London: Phillimore, 1898, p.91-106.

KITTISFORD

SEAGER, H. W., ed. 'Marriages at Kittisford, 1695 to 1812', in BLAGG, Thos. M., & PHILLIMORE, W. P. W., eds. Somerset parish registers: marriages, 14. P.P.R.S., 170. London: Phillimore, 1913, p.61-4.

See also Chipstable

LANGFORD BUDVILLE

SEAGER, H. W., ed. 'Marriages at Langford Budville, 1607 to 1812', in PHILLIMORE, W. P. W., & SEAGER, H. W., eds. Somerset parish registers: marriages, 8. P.P.R.S., 68. London: Phillimore, 1906, p.121-40.

LANGPORT

'Marriages at Langport, 1728 to 1812', in PHILLIMORE, W. P. W., & HAYWARD, Douglas L, eds. Somerset parish registers: marriages, 1. P.P.R.S., 5. London: Phillimore, 1898, p.149-59.

LILSTOCK

BELL, W. A., ed. 'Marriages at Lilstock, 1661 to 1812', in PHILLIMORE, W. P. W., & BELL, W. A., eds. Somerset parish registers: marriages, 12. P.P.R.S., 122. London: Phillimore, 1910, p.167-70.

LIMINGTON

BINNEY, D. B., ed. 'Marriages at Limington, 1695 to 1812', in PHILLIMORE, W. P. W., & HAYWARD, Douglas L, eds. Somerset parish registers: marriages, 2. P.P.R.S., 7. London: Phillimore, 1899, p.25-9.

LONG LOAD

'Marriages at Long Load, 1749 to 1808, in PHILLIMORE, W. P. W., & ROSS, D. M., eds., Somerset parish registers: marriages, 3. P.P.R.S., 23. London: Phillimore, 1901, p.11-12.

LONG SUTTON

'Marriages at Long Sutton, 1559 to 1812', in PHILLIMORE, W. P. W., & HAYWARD, Douglas L, eds. Somerset parish registers: marriages, 1. P.P.R.S., 5. London: Phillimore, 1898, p.107-33.

LOPEN

SEAGER, H. W., ed. 'Marriages at Lopen, 1723 to 1812', in PHILLIMORE, W. P. W., & SEAGER, H. W., eds. Somerset parish registers: marriages, 13. P.P.R.S., 131. London: Phillimore, 1910, p.13-19.

MARTOCK

ROSS, D. M., ed. 'Marriages at Martock, 1559-1812', in PHILLIMORE, W. P. W., & ROSS, D. M., eds., Somerset parish registers: marriages, 3. P.P.R.S., 23. London: Phillimore, 1901.

MIDSOMER NORTON

HOLMYARD, E. J., ed. 'Marriages at Midsomer Norton, 1701 to 1837', in BLAGG, Thos. M., & PHILLIMORE, W. P. W., eds. Somerset parish registers: marriages, 14. P.P.R.S., 170. London: Phillimore, 1913, p.105-38.

MILBORNE PORT

MAYO, C. H. 'Parish registers of Milborne Port, Somerset', N.Q.S.D., 2, 1891, p.143-52 & 178-89. [Notes on the registers, including a few extracts]

MILVERTON

SEAGER, H. W., ed. 'Marriages at Milverton, 1538 to 1812', in PHILLIMORE, W. P. W., & SEAGER, H. W., eds. Somerset parish registers: marriages, 13. P.P.R.S., 131. London: Phillimore, 1910, p.91-170.

MUCHELNEY

'Marriages at Muchelney, 1703 to 1812', in PHILLIMORE, W. P. W., & HAYWARD, Douglas L, eds. Somerset parish registers: marriages, 1. P.P.R.S., 5. London: Phillimore, 1898, p.135-9.

MUDFORD

BATES-HARBIN, E. H. 'Notes on Mudford register, Somerset, vol. 1 (1563-1638)', N.Q.S.D., 13, 1913, p.217-20. [Note, with a handful of extracts]

NETHER STOWEY

BELL, W. A., ed. 'Marriages at Nether Stowey, 1645 to 1812', in PHILLIMORE, W. P. W., & BELL, W. A., eds. Somerset parish registers: marriages, 12. P.P.R.S., 122. London: Phillimore, 1910, p.43-60.

NORTH CADBURY

JONES, I. F. 'The reliability of parish registers', Genealogists' magazine, 9(4), 1941, p.130-1. [Includes examples, 1695, from North Cadbury]

JONES, I. Fitzroy. 'The earliest North Cadbury register', N.Q.S.D., 21, 1935, p.245-50. [Notes only]

NORTH CURRY

OLIVEY, Hugh P., ed. 'Marriages at North Curry, 1539 to 1812', in PHILLIMORE, W. P. W., & HAYWARD, Douglas L, eds. Somerset parish registers: marriages, 2. P.P.R.S., 7. London: Phillimore, 1899, p.75-139.

NORTHOVER

'Marrriages at Northover, 1531 to 1812', in PHILLIMORE, W. P. W., & HAYWARD, Douglas L, eds. Somerset parish registers: marriages, 1. P.P.R.S., 5. London: Phillimore, 1898, p.141-7.

BATES, E. H. 'Date of Northover register', N.Q.S.D., 7, 1901, p.113-4. [Discussion of the date on which the register commenced]

See also Bath

NORTH PETHERTON

DWELLY, E., ed. North Petherton registers, annotated with the bishops transcripts at Wells. Dwelly's parish records, 10-13 & 15. Fleet, Hants: E. Dwelly, 1922-6.

NORTON FITZWARREN

SEAGER, H. W., ed. 'Marriages at Norton Fitzwarren, 1565 to 1812', in PHILLIMORE, W. P. W., & SEAGER, H. W., eds. Somerset parish registers: marriages, 8. P.P.R.S., 68. London: Phillimore, 1906, p.85-104.

NYNEHEAD

SEAGER, H. W., ed. 'Marriages at Nynehead, 1670 to 1812', in PHILLIMORE, W. P. W., & SEAGER, H. W., eds. Somerset parish registers: marriages, 8. P.P.R.S., 68. London: Phillimore, 1906, p.141-50.

ORCHARD PORTMAN

SEAGER, H. W., ed. 'Marriages at Orchard Portman, 1538 to 1812', in PHILLIMORE, W. P. W., & SEAGER, H. W., eds. Somerset parish registers: marriages, 7. P.P.R.S., 69. London: Phillimore, 1905, p.69-78.

OTHERY

See Bath

OTTERFORD

SEAGER, H. W., ed. 'Marriages at Otterford, 1588 to 1812', in PHILLIMORE, W. P. W., & SEAGER, H. W., eds. Somerset parish registers: marriages, 11. P.P.R.S., 114. London: Phillimore, 1906, p.125-33.

OTTERHAMPTON

BELL, W. A., ed. 'Marriages at Otterhampton, 1656 to 1749', in PHILLIMORE, W. P. W., BELL, W. A., & WHISTLER, C. W., eds. Somerset parish registers: marriages, 6. P.P.R.S., 54. London: Phillimore, 1905, p.51-3.

OVERSTOWEY

BELL, W. A., ed. 'Marriages at Overstowey, 1558 to 1812', in PHILLIMORE, W. P. W., BELL, W. A., & WHISTLER, C. W., eds. Somerset parish registers: marriages, 6. P.P.R.S., 54. London: Phillimore, 1905, p.55-72.

PITCOMBE

See Chipstable

PITMINSTER

EASTWOOD, Arthur, ed. 'Marriages at Pitminster, 1542 to 1812', in PHILLIMORE, W. P. W., & SEAGER, H. W., eds. Somerset parish registers: marriages, 7. P.P.R.S., 69. London: Phillimore, 1905, p.7-64.

PITNEY

'Marriages at Pitney, 1623 to 1812', in PHILLIMORE, W. P. W., & HAYWARD, Douglas L, eds. Somerset parish registers: marriages, 2. P.P.R.S., 7. London: Phillimore, 1899, p.1-24.

HAYWARD, Douglas L. 'Pitney and its register book', S.A.N.H.S., 37(2), 1891, p.92-99. [General discussion, with a few extracts]

PODYMORE MILTON

'Marriages at Podymore Milton, 1744 to 1812', in PHILLIMORE, W. P. W., & HAYWARD, Douglas L, eds. Somerset parish registers: marriages, 2. P.P.R.S., 7. London: Phillimore, 1899, p.31-33.

'Quakers in Somerset', N.Q.S.D., 17, 1923, p.111-2. See also p.174-8. [Extracts from Podymore Milton parish register, 17-18th c.]

PUCKINGTON

BATES, E. H., ed. 'Marriages at Puckington, 1695 to 1812', in PHILLIMORE, W. P. W., & BATES, E. H., eds. Somerset parish registers: marriages, 4. P.P.R.S., 30. London: Phillimore, 1902, p.143-50.

RADDINGTON

See Bath and Chipstable

RUISHTON

SEAGER, H. W., ed. 'Marriages at Ruishton, 1679 to 1812', in PHILLIMORE, W. P. W., & SEAGER, H. W., eds. Somerset parish registers: marriages, 8. P.P.R.S., 68. London: Phillimore, 1906, p.45-9.

RUNNINGTON

SEAGER, H. W., ed. 'Marriages at Runnington, 1586 to 1812', in PHILLIMORE, W. P. W., & SEAGER, H. W., eds. Somerset parish registers: marriages, 11. P.P.R.S., 114. London: Phillimore, 1906, p.125-33.

ST. MICHAEL CHURCH

BARTLETT, R. Grosvenor. The registers of St. Michael Church, Co. Somerset, 1695-1812. Parish Register Society, 72. London: the Society, 1914.

SAMPFORD ARUNDEL

SEAGER, H. W., ed. 'Marriages at Sampford Arundel, 1698 to 1812', in PHILLIMORE, W. P. W., & SEAGER, H. W., eds. Somerset parish registers: marriages, 11. P.P.R.S., 114. London: Phillimore, 1906, p.143-9.

SHEPTON BEAUCHAMP

LETHBRIDGE, A., ed. 'Marriages at Shepton Beauchamp, 1558 to 1812', in PHILLIMORE, W. P. W., & BATES, E. H., eds. Somerset parish registers: marriages, 4. P.P.R.S., 30. London: Phillimore, 1902, p.85-105.

SOMERTON

'Marriages at Somerton, 1697 to 1812', in PHILLIMORE, W. P. W., & HAYWARD, Douglas L, eds. Somerset parish registers: marriages, 2. P.P.R.S., 7. London: Phillimore, 1899, p.35-68.

SOUTH BARROW

See Ash Priors

SPAXTON

BELL, W. A., ed. 'Marriages at Spaxton, 1558 to 1812', in PHILLIMORE, W. P. W., BELL, W. A., & WHISTLER, C. W., eds. Somerset parish registers: marriages, 6. P.P.R.S., 54. London: Phillimore, 1905, p.129-50.

STAPLE FITZPAINE

SEAGER, H. W., ed. 'Marriages at Staple Fitzpaine and Bickenhall, 1682 to 1812', in PHILLIMORE, W. P. W., & SEAGER, H. W., eds. Somerset parish registers: marriages, 13. P.P.R.S., 131. London: Phillimore, 1910, p.1-12.

STOCKLAND GAUNTS

WHISTLER, C. W., ed. 'Marriages at Stockland Gaunts (otherwise Stockland Bristol), 1538 to 1807', in PHILLIMORE, W. P. W., BELL, W. A., & WHISTLER, C. W., eds. Somerset parish registers: marriages, 6. P.P.R.S., 54. London: Phillimore, 1905, p.55-72.

STOCKLINCH MAGDALEN

POWELL, W. B., ed. 'Marriages at Stocklinch Magdalen, 1712 to 1776', in PHILLIMORE, W. P. W., & BATES, E. H., eds. Somerset parish registers: marriages, 4. P.P.R.S., 30. London: Phillimore, 1902, p.63-4.

STOCKLINCH OTTERSAY

POOLE, R. B., ed. 'Marriages at Stocklinch Ottersay, 1558 to 1812', in PHILLIMORE, W. P. W., & BATES, E. H., eds. Somerset parish registers: marriages, 4. P.P.R.S., 30. London: Phillimore, 1902, p.65-73.

STOGURSEY

BELL, W. A., ed. 'Marriages at Stogursey, 1595 to 1812', in PHILLIMORE, W. P. W., & BELL, W. A., eds. Somerset parish registers: marriages, 12. P.P.R.S., 122. London: Phillimore, 1910, p.1-41.

STOKE ST. MARY

SEAGER, H. W., ed. 'Marriages at Stoke St. Mary, 1679 to 1812', in PHILLIMORE, W. P. W., & SEAGER, H. W., eds. Somerset parish registers: marriages, 7. P.P.R.S., 69. London: Phillimore, 1905, p.79-83.

STOWELL

MAYO, C. H. 'Parish register of Stowell, Somerset', N.Q.S.D., 3, 1893, p.4-8. [Includes some entries, 1574-1678]

STREET

JEWERS, Arthur J. The parish registers of Street, in the county of Somerset. Baptisms and marriages to 1755. Burials to 1762. Exeter: William Pollard, 1898. [Supplement to the Genealogist, N.S., 11-13.]

STRINGSTON

BELL, W. A., ed. 'Marriages at Stringston, 1634 to 1812', in PHILLIMORE, W. P. W., & BELL, W. A., eds. Somerset parish registers: marriages, 12. P.P.R.S., 122. London: Phillimore, 1910, p.157-60.

SWELL

RIGBYE, J., ed. 'Marriages at Swell, 1559 to 1812', in PHILLIMORE, W. P. W., & BATES, E. H., eds. Somerset parish registers: marriages, 4. P.P.R.S., 30. London: Phillimore, 1902, p.151-9.

'Marriages at Swell, 1713 to 1754', in PHILLIMORE, W. P. W., & ROSS, D. M., eds. Somerset parish registers: marriages, 5. P.P.R.S., 49. London: Phillimore, 1904, p.113-6.

TAUNTON (ST. JAMES)

'Marriages at Taunton, St. James, 1610 to 1837', in SEAGER, H. W., ed. Somerset parish registers, 15, P.P.R.S., 222. London: Phillimore, 1915.

TAUNTON (ST. MARY MAGDALENE)

SEAGER, H. W., ed. 'Marriages at Taunton, St. Mary Magdalene, 1558-1812', in PHILLIMORE, W. P. W., & SEAGER, H. W., eds. Somerset parish registers: marriages, 9. P.P.R.S., 85. London: Phillimore, 1907, p.1-160. [Pt.1. 1558-1727]

BATES, E. H., ed. 'Marriages at Taunton, St. Mary Magdalene', in PHILLIMORE, W. P. W., SEAGER, H. W., & BATES, E. H., eds. Somerset parish registers: marriages, 10. P.P.R.S., 88. London: Phillimore, 1906, p.1-113. [Pt.2: 1728-1812]

TEMPLECOMBE

B., J. 'Templecombe register', N.Q.S.D., 5, 1897-8, p.91-2. [Note with brief extracts from the register]

THORNE FAULCON

SEAGER, H. W., ed. 'Marriages at Thorne Faulcon, 1720 to 1812', in PHILLIMORE, W. P. W., & SEAGER, H. W., eds. Somerset parish registers: marriages, 8. P.P.R.S., 68. London: Phillimore, 1906, p.19-24.

THORNE ST. MARGARET

SEAGER, H. W., ed. 'Marriages at Thorne St. Margaret, 1721 to 1812', in PHILLIMORE, W. P. W., & SEAGER, H. W., eds. Somerset parish registers: marriages, 11. P.P.R.S., 114. London: Phillimore, 1906, p.151-2.

THURLBEAR

SEAGER, H. W., ed. 'Marriages at Thurlbear, 1700 to 1812', in PHILLIMORE, W. P. W., & SEAGER, H. W., eds. Somerset parish registers: marriages, 7. P.P.R.S., 69. London: Phillimore, 1905, p.85-91.

THURLOXTON

BELL, W. A., ed. 'Marriages at Thurloxton, 1559 to 1812', in PHILLIMORE, W. P. W., & BELL, W. A., eds. Somerset parish registers: marriages, 12. P.P.R.S., 122. London: Phillimore, 1910, p.149-56.

TRULL

SEAGER, H. W., ed. 'Marriages at Trull, 1671 to 1744', in PHILLIMORE, W. P. W., & SEAGER, H. W., eds. Somerset parish registers: marriages, 7. P.P.R.S., 69. London: Phillimore, 1905, p.93-105.

WEDMORE

HERVEY, S. H. A. Wedmore parish registers, marriages, 1561-1839. 3 vols. Wells: Jackson, 1888-90. [v.1. Baptisms, 1561-1812. v.2. Marriages, 1561-1839. v.3. Burials, 1561-1860]

WELLINGTON

SEAGER, H. W., ed. 'Marriages at Wellington, 1683 to 1812', in PHILLIMORE, W. P. W., & SEAGER, H. W., eds. Somerset parish registers: marriages, 11. P.P.R.S., 114. London: Phillimore, 1906, p.1-105.

WEST BAGBOROUGH

SEAGER, H. W., ed. 'Marriages at West Bagborough, 1565 to 1812', in BLAGG, Thos. M., & PHILLIMORE, W. P. W., eds. Somerset parish registers: marriages, 14. P.P.R.S., 170. London: Phillimore, 1913, p.25-45.

WEST BUCKLAND

SEAGER, H. W., ed. 'Marriages at West Buckland, 1538 to 1812', in PHILLIMORE, W. P. W., & SEAGER, H. W., eds. Somerset parish registers: marriages, 8. P.P.R.S., 68. London: Phillimore, 1906, p.51-74.

WEST HATCH

'Marriages at West Hatch, 1604 to 1812', in PHILLIMORE, W. P. W., & ROSS, D. M., eds., Somerset parish registers: marriages, 3. P.P.R.S., 23. London: Phillimore, 1901, p.1-10.

WEST MONKTON

SEAGER, H. W., ed. 'Marriages at West Monkton, 1710 to 1812', in PHILLIMORE, W. P. W., & SEAGER, H. W., eds. Somerset parish registers: marriages, 8. P.P.R.S., 68. London: Phillimore, 1906, p.25-44.

WEST QUANTOXHEAD

'Extract from the register of West Quantoxhead, Co. Somerset', Genealogist, 3, 1879, p.26-30 & 46-51. [Concerning Conibeare, Palmer, Evans, and other families]

WESTON SUPER MARE

KNIGHT, F. H., ed. 'Marriages at Weston-Super-Mare, 1682 to 1837', in BLAGG, Thos. M., & PHILLIMORE, W. P. W., eds. Somerset parish registers: marriages, 14. P.P.R.S., 170. London: Phillimore, 1913, p.139-48.

WHITELACKINGTON

BUCKLAND, J. V., ed. 'Marriages at White-lackington, 1695 to 1837', in PHILLIMORE, W. P. W., & SEAGER, H. W., eds. Somerset parish registers: marriages, 13. P.P.R.S., 131. London: Phillimore, 1910, p.21-8.

WHITESTAUNTON

CARTWRIGHT, H. A., ed. 'Marriages at Whitestaunton, 1606 to 1811', in PHILLIMORE, W. P. W., & BATES, E. H., eds. Somerset parish registers: marriages, 4. P.P.R.S., 30. London: Phillimore, 1902, p.51-62.

WILTON

SPENCER, Joseph Houghton. A copy of the registers of the baptisms, marriages and burials at the church of St. George, in the parish of Wilton, adjoining Taunton in the county of Somerset, from A.D. 1558 to A.D. 1837. Taunton: Barnicott and Son, 1890.

WINSHAM

See Combe St. Nicholas

WRAXALL

WERE, F., ed. 'Marriages at Wraxall, 1562 to 1812', in PHILLIMORE, W. P. W., & BATES, E. H., eds. Somerset parish registers: marriages, 4. P.P.R.S., 30. London: Phillimore, 1902, p.125-42.

WRINGTON

SCARTH, Preb. 'Ancient register of Wrington church', Proceedings of the Bath Natural History & Antiquarian Field Club, 6, 1873, p.436-44.

See also South Barrow

YEOVIL

GOODCHILD, John. 'Commonwealth banns in Yeovil', N.Q.S.D., 18, 1926, p.113-5. [In book of 1653]

YEOVILTON

HYSON, J. B., ed. 'Marriages at Yeovilton, 1655 to 1812', in PHILLIMORE, W. P. W., & HAYWARD, Douglas L., eds. Somerset parish registers: marriages, 2. P.P.R.S., 7. London: Phillimore, 1899, p.69-73.

CHAPTER 9
PROBATE RECORDS AND
INQUISITIONS POST MORTEM

Probate records - wills, inventories, accounts, bonds, etc - are an invaluable source of genealogical information. Many researchers have compiled abstracts and indexes of Somerset wills. Surveys are provided by:

HUMPHREYS, A. L. 'Somerset-shire wills', Notes & queries, 185, 1943, p.303-8.

MEDLYCOTT, Mervyn. 'Somerset wills', G.T., 10(1), 1984/5, p.34-5. [Discusses his efforts to trace 15,000 wills from the Diocese of Bath & Wells, with much useful information on locations]

MONDAY, Alfred James. 'Extracts from some Somerset wills', S.A.N.H.S., 31(2), 1885, p.20-32.

NATIONAL SOCIETY OF THE COLONIAL DAMES OF AMERICA IN THE COMMONWEALTH OF VIRGINIA. LYNCHBERG COMMITTEE. Index to wills, county of Somerset, England. [Lynchberg, Virginia]: the Committee, 1963.

There are many lists, indexes, and abstracts of Somerset wills. Unfortunately, all probate records for the Diocese of Bath & Wells were destroyed in the Exeter Probate Registry bombing in 1942. An attempt to mitigate the effects of this disaster was made by the Somerset Record Society:

RAWLINS, S. W., & JONES, I. Fitzroy, eds. Somerset wills from Exeter. Somerset Record Society, 62. Taunton: the Society, 1952.

A major collection of abstracts from wills was made in the nineteenth century by Rev. Frederick Brown. See:

CRISP, Frederick Arthur, ed. Abstracts of Somerset wills, etc., copied from the manuscript collections of the late Rev. Frederick Brown ... 6 vols. London: F.A. Crisp, 1887-1890.

Crisp only prints a selection from Brown's collection, Further information, including a surname index, is provided by:

FRY, Edw. Alex. 'A description of the Rev. Frederick Brown's collection of manuscript Somerset wills and pedigrees now preserved at Taunton Castle', S.A.N.H.S., 57(2), 1911, p.86-90.

Other printed abstracts of Somerset wills include:

WEAVER, F. W., ed. Somerset medieval wills. Somerset Record Society, 16, 19, & 21. Taunton: the Society, 1901-5. Reprinted Gloucester: Alan Sutton, 1983. [Series 1: 1383-1500 (from the Prerogative Court of Canterbury). Series 2: 1501-1530, with some Somerset wills preserved at Lambeth (i.e. for 1363-1491). Series 3: 1531-1558]

HILTON, Dorothy O., & HOLWORTHY, Richard, ed. Medieval wills from Wells deposited in the diocesan registry, Wells, 1543 to 1546 and 1554 to 1556. Somerset Record Society, 40. Taunton: the Society, 1925.

WEAVER, F. W., ed. 'Wells wills: [Serel collection]', S.A.N.H.S., 61(2), 1916, p.54-104. [Abstracts of 150 wills, 1539-41]

WEAVER, F. W., ed. Wells wills, arranged in parishes and annotated. London: Kegan Paul, Trench, Trubner & Co., 1890. [1528-36]

See also

WEAVER, F. W. 'Some early wills at Wells District Probate Registry', Downside review, 13, 1894, p.273-9, & 14, 1895, p.10-21. Reprinted as Some early wills. Yeovil: Western Chronicle, 1895.

Abstracts of Wellington wills are included in:

HUMPHREYS, A. L. Materials for the history of the town and parish of Wellington in the county of Somerset. London: H. Gray, 1908-1914. [Pt.1. Wills (Wellington & West Buckland) 1372-1811). Pt. 2. Manorial court rolls, 1277-1908. Pt. 3. Nonconformist history: the Independents. Pt. 4. Nonconformist history: the Baptists.]

BATES HARBIN, E. H. 'Muniments of Woborne Almshouse, Yeovil', N.Q.S.D.,15, 1917, p.275-9, & 16, 1920, p.29-31. [Wills of John Trock, 1400, Stephen Paco, 1401, Robert Boton, 1406, & John Sparkeford, 1388]

CROSS, J. 'Somerset and Dorset folk in Essex', N.Q.S.D., 6, 1899, p.175. [Abstracts of wills: Berkeley, Horsey, Wilder and Courteys]

COLEMAN, James. 'Four Wells wills of the 14th century', N.Q.S.D., 8, 1903, p.21-3, 52-4, 151-3, & 196. [Richard of Chipmanslade, 1311; John Hywysch, 1361; Nicholas de Pontesbury, 1371; John Gy of Wells, 1377]

A number of indexes to the destroyed wills at least tell you that a will once existed. For those proved in the Archdeaconry of Taunton, see:

FRY, Edward Alexander, ed. Calendar of wills and administrations in the court of the Archdeacon of Taunton (parts I & II, wills only), 1537-1799. Index Library, 45. London: British Record Society, 1912. See also: PHIPPS, H. R. 'Somerset testamentary documents hitherto unlisted', Genealogists' magazine, 5(10), 1931, p.328-36.

Administrations from the same court, and wills from the royal peculiar of Ilminster, are indexed in:

FRY, Edward Alexander, ed. Calendar of wills and administrations in the court of the Archdeacon of Taunton (Part III, Administrations), 1596-1799, and (part IV), Calendar of wills in the royal peculiar of Ilminster, 1690-1857. Index Library, 45a (sometimes bound with vol.53). London: British Record Society, 1921.

Other published lists include:

'Wills proved in the Deanery of Wells, 1558', N.Q.S.D., 7, 1901, p.324-5.

MARKS, Arthur W. 'Somerset medieval wills and other records at Canterbury', N.Q.S.D., 24, 1946, p.273-6. [Includes list of wills, 1500-1]

Somerset wills were also occasionally proved in the Diocese of Bristol; these wills may be consulted. The jurisdiction of the Bristol Diocese Consistory Court extended to the Somerset parishes of Abbots Leigh, St. Mary Redcliff, & Temple, otherwise St. Cross. For an index, see:

FRY, Edward Alexander, ed. Calendar of wills proved in the Consistory Court (City and Deanery of Bristol Division) of the Diocese of Bristol, 1572-1792, and also a calendar of wills in the Great Orphan Books preserved in the Council House, Bristol, 1379-1674. Index Library, 17. London: British Record Society, 1897.

See also:

MAYO, C. H. 'Calendar of wills in the archives of the Dean and Chapter of Bristol', N.Q.S.D., 13, 1913, p.153-6.

A few Somerset administrations are listed in:

FRY, G. S. 'Dorset administrations', N.Q.S.D., 4, 1894-5, p.146-9, 213-5, & 250-3.

For a general discussion of Bridgwater wills, see:

DILKS, T. B. 'Bridgwater wills, 1310-1497', S.A.N.H.S., 66(2), 1920, p.78-97.

A number of wills for particular individuals and families have been published. See:

AVERY

JEWERS, A. J. 'Avery family', N.Q.S.D., 5, 1897-8, p.277. [Will of Joan Avery of Frome Selwood, 1683]

AVILL

L., H. M. 'An early Somerset will', N.Q.S.D., 16, 1920, p.48-9. [Richard of Avill, 1307]

BABER

JEWERS, A. J. 'Baber family', N.Q.S.D., 5, 1897-8, p.176-80. [Wills; see also p.218 for monumental inscriptions]

BALAM

LONGDEN, H. Isham. 'Balam and Isham of Isle Brewers, Co. Somerset', N.Q.S.D., 4, 1894-5, p.85. [Wills of William Balam of Isle Brewers, 1502, & Alexander Balam of Barton Mills, Suffolk, 1544]

BAVE

POYNTON, F. J. 'Evidence from wills supporting the pedigree of Bave', M.G.H., 2nd series, 1, 1886, p.254-8 & 262-5. [Bave wills, 17-18th c.]

BICKNELL

MONDAY, A. J. 'The last will and testament of Dame Elizabeth Biconyll, widow of Sir John Biconyll [or Bicknell], knight', S.A.N.H.S., 39(2), 1893, p.35-42. [1500]

BOWER

WEINSTOCK, M. B. 'Inventory of goods of Adrian Bower of Wraxall', N.Q.S.D., 26, 1955, p.232-6. [1693]

BUBWITH

C., C. M. 'Will of Nicholas Bubwith, Bishop of Bath and Wells', N.Q.S.D., 8, 1903, p.28-31. [1424]

CARSLEIGH

BARTELOT, R. Grosvenor. 'Peter Carsleigh of Winscombe, Somerset', N.Q.S.D., 14, 1915, p.177. [Will, 1534]

CHILD

ORLEBAR, G. 'Child wills', M.G.H., 5th series, 6, 1926-8, p.413-9. [Includes wills of Richard Childe of Wrington, 1582, & William Childes of Wrington, 1634]

CRANE

MONDAY, Alfred Jas. 'Crane family', N.Q.S.D., 4, 1894-5, p.210-3. [Includes extracts from will of Francis Crane of Bridgwater, 1719]

D'ACTON
'Richard D'Acton's will', N.Q.S.D., 7, 1901, p.260-2. [1388]

DANIEL
CUNNINGHAM, Peter, ed. 'Will of Samuel Daniel, the poet, Shakespeare's rival and contemporary', Shakespeare Society's papers, 4, 1849, p.156-8. [Of Beckington; 1619]

DAUBENEY
'Sir Giles Daubeney's will, 1445', N.Q.S.D., 1, 1890, p.243-6.

DODINGTON
MARSHALL, George W. 'Genealogical notices of the family of Dodington, of Dodington, Co. Somerset', Reliquary, 15, 1874-5, p.86-90. [Will of George Dodington, 1618, with pedigree]

DUGDALE
'James Dugdale', N.Q.S.D., 13, 1913, p.79-81. [Will, 1661; vicar of Evercreech]

FUSSELL
DANIEL, F. de F. 'Will of William Fussell of Horsington, Somerset, 7th September, 1668', N.Q.S.D., 28, 1968, p.68-9. [Includes probate inventory]

GODDARD
GODDARD, R. W. K. 'Goddard wills', M.G.H., 4th series, 2, 1908, p.289-92 & 327-34; 3, 1910, p.6-9 69-72, 123-6, 162-5; 210-14, 263-7, 293-7, & 360-3; 4, 1912, p.11-15, 85-9, 103-7, 183-90, 231-8 & 252-69. [Includes wills from many Southern counties, including Somerset]

GORGES
MASTER, George S. 'Some Gorges wills', Proceedings of the Clifton Antiquarian Club, 4, 1900, p.241-51.

GYLLETT
'William Gyllett, rector of Chaffcombe', N.Q.S.D., 17, 1923, p.121. See also 22, 1938, p.135-7. [Probate inventory, 1641]

HARINGTON
'Abstract of wills relating to the family of Harington', M.G.H., N.S., 3, 1880, p.228-9.

HARVIE
MONDAY, Alfred Jas. 'The wills of two Somerset priests ...', N.Q.S.D., 5, 1897-8, p.140-1. [John Harvie, 1540, & Alexander Magot, 1558]

HEYRON
WEAVER, F. W. 'The Heyron chantry in the church of All Saints, Langport', S.A.N.H.S., 40, 1894, p.70-5. [Includes wills of Richard Langport, 1490, John Heyron, 1501, & John Heyron, junior, 1507]

HILLIARD
'William Hilliard of Sea, esquire', N.Q.S.D., 8, 1903, p.3-8. [Probate inventory, 1668]

HOLE
NEVILL, E. R. 'The will of John Hole, 1618', N.Q.S.D., 15, 1917, p.214-5. [Of Galhampton]

HORNER
'The will in brief of Thomas Horner of Cloford, esq', M.G.H., N.S., 4, 1884, p.165. [1611]

HULLS
NEVILL, Edmund. 'Hulls of Closeworth, Somerset, and Beaminster, Halstock and Corscombe, Dorset', N.Q.S.D., 11, 1909, p.174-6. [Wills]

JONES
'A will of 1496: bequest to the Guild of Merchants', N.Q.S.D., 24, 1946, p.174-5. [John Jones of Milborne Port]

KING

MONDAY, A. J. 'Will of a Taunton merchant in the reign of Elizabeth', <u>Western antiquary</u>, 5(10), 261-2. [Roger King, 1579]

KNIGHT

KNIGHT, Francis. 'Knight family', <u>N.Q.S.D.</u>, 17, 1923, p.98-9. [Will of James Knight, of Broomfield, 1679]

LANE

'Will of the Rev. John Lane', <u>N.Q.S.D.</u>, 17, 1923, p.119. [1540]

LANGLEY

Serrell, D. H. 'The curious will of a Wincanton man', <u>N.Q.S.D.</u>, 7, 1900, p32-3. [John Langley, 1651]

LEVERSEGGE

LIGHT, M. E. 'Will of William Leversegge of Valleis, Frome Selwood, esq....', <u>N.Q.S.D.</u>, 5, 1897-8, p.300-1. [1582]

LONG

'Will of Robert Long, 1669', <u>M.G.H.</u>, N.S., 3, 1880, p.104-7. [Of Staunton Prior]

MAGOT

See Harvie

MARKS

MARKS, Arthur W. 'Will of Anne Marks', <u>N.Q.S.D.</u>, 23, 1942, p.153-4. [Of Yeovil, 1754]

MESSETER

'Will of Richarde Messeter', <u>N.Q.S.D.</u>, 25, 1950, p.135-8. [Of Cranmore, 1536]

NORTH

PEDEN, Joan. 'The cost of dying, 1696', <u>N.Q.S.D.</u>, 30, 1974-9, p.217-9. [Extracts from Mary North of Churchstanton's will and executor's account]

POMEROY

MONDAY, A. J. 'A curious clause in the will of Ralph Pomeroy of the parish of 'Saint Cuthbrts' [Cuthberts] in Wells, 'shoomaker', <u>Western Antiquary.</u>, 3, 1884, p.236.

PORTMAN

'The personalty of Sir William Portman, Baronet, K.B.', <u>N.Q.S.D.</u>, 13, 1913, p.320-5. [Inventory, 1690; of Orchard Portman]

PYM

MONDAY, A. J. 'The will of a Somersetshire yeoman in the reign of Queen Elizabeth', <u>Western antiquary</u>, 3, 1884, p.225-6. [John Pym of Kilton, 1565]

ROSE

McGARVIE, Michael. 'The will of Edith Rose of Marston Bigot, 1587', <u>N.Q.S.D.</u>, 32, 1986- , p.627.

RUSSELL

THOMPSON, E. M. 'An early Somerset will', N.Q.S.D., 6, 1899, p.359-60. [Will of Isabella Russell, widow of John Chyehaye, 1361]

SAGITTARY

FRY, George S. 'Frederick Sagittary, D.M.' <u>N.Q.S.D.</u>, 15, 1917, P.200-3. See also p.181-2. [Sagittary wills, 17-18th c.]

SCUTTE

'Wills in brief of Scutte, of Stanton Drew, Co. Somerset', <u>M.G.H.</u>, N.S., 4, 1884, p.165. [1557 & 1589]

SMITH

BROOKE, L. E. J. 'Yeovil household goods, 1520', <u>N.Q.S.D.</u>, 32, 1986- , p.614-9. [List of goods bequeathed by John Smith, & auctioned by the churchwardens, with the names of purchasers]

STAYNINGS

'Will of Charles Staynings of Holnycote, Co. Somerset, 1693', M.G.H., N.S., 3, 1880, p.20-22.

STRODE

'Strode of Shepton Mallet', N.Q.S.D., 1, 1890, p.236-7 & 252-3. See also p.262-3. [Wills of Jeffery Upton, 1582, Jeffery Strode, 1624/5, Sir George Strode, 1662, John Strode, 1686, Thomas Cullum, 1717, & John Hyde, 1723]

TANNER

McGARVIE, Michael. 'A will proved in the Peculiar Court of Witham Friary', N.Q.S.D., 30, 1974-9, p.450-1. [Extracts from will of Edward Tanner of Witham Friary, 1806]

THORNTON

BATES, E. H. 'Will of Henry Thornton, 1533', N.Q.S.D., 7, 1901, p.111-3.

UPTON

UPTON, W. H. 'Upton: abstracts of wills and records of administration', M.G.H., 2nd series, 2, 1888, p.318-24, 350-51; 3, 1890, p.31-2, 47-8, 94-6, 111-2, 156-7, 163-8, 188-91.

VENNER

'Will of Tobias Venner, M.D.', Proceedings of the Bath Natural History and Antiquarian Field Club, 3, 1877, p.11. [1659]

WILLIAMS

DANIEL, F. de F. 'Will of John Williams, rector of Abbas and Temple Combe, 23rd March, 1692', N.Q.S.D., 28, 1968, p.39-40. [Includes probate inventory]

'Inventory of goods of John Williams of South Cheriton', N.Q.S.D., 26, 1955, p.165-7. [1693]

WITHERS

'Early Withers wills proved at Taunton', N.Q.S.D., 15, 1917, p.143-4 & 167-9. [16th c.]

YOUNG

MONDAY, A. J. 'On two Somerset wills, temp Edward VI', S.A.N.H.S., 29(2), 1883, p.61-8. [Thomas Young of Kingsbrompton, & Richard Yea of Wiveliscombe]

Inquisitions Post Mortem

Inquisitions post mortem are invaluable sources of genealogical information, and are particularly useful for tracing the descent of manors. They were taken on the death of tenants in chief, and record lands held in chief, with the names of heirs. Those for Somerset are listed in:

FRY, Edward Alexander. 'On the inquisitiones post mortem for Somerset from Henry III to Richard III (1216-1485)', S.A.N.H.S., 44(2), 1898, p.79-148.

FRY, Edward Alexander. 'On the inquisitions post mortem for Somerset from Henry VII to Charles I (1485-1649)', S.A.N.H.S., 47(2), 1901, p.1-122.

Many inquisitions post mortem are included in:

HAWKINS, Michael James, ed. Sales of wards in Somerset, 1603-1641. Somerset Record Society, 67. Taunton: the Society, 1965.

See also:

M. 'Abstract of inquisitions post mortem, temp Hen III, for the counties of Somerset and Dorset [Ms. Harl. 4120]', Collectanea topographica et genealogica, 2, 1835, p.48-56.

A number of inquisitions post
mortem have been separately
published:

COTEL

'Cotel', <u>Genealogist</u>, 1,
1877, p.340-4. [1337]

DODDERIDGE

DODDERIDGE, S. E. 'John
Dodridge of Stogumber',
<u>N.Q.S.D</u>., 19, 1929, p.190-1.
[1621]

STOURTON

V[IVIAN]-N[EAL], A. W. 'Glass
at West Bower, in the parish
of Durleigh', <u>N.Q.S.D</u>., 27,
1961, p.5-6. [Margaret Stourton,
1490]

CHAPTER 10

MONUMENTAL INSCRIPTIONS

Monumental inscriptions are an important source of genealogical information, especially for the nineteenth and twentieth centuries. A general discussion of the monuments in the county is provided in:

WICKHAM, A. K. Churches of Somerset. New ed. Dawlish: David & Charles; London: Macdonald, 1965.

See also:

HARDIMAN, W. 'Somerset epitaphs: quaint, curious, and pathetic', S.A.N.H.S., 31(2), 1885, p.20-32.

The standard guide to brasses is:

CONNOR, Arthur B. Monumental brasses in Somerset. Bath: Kingswood Reprints, 1970. Reprinted from S.A.N.H.S., 1931-53.

See also:

SADLER, A. G. The indents of lost monumental brasses in Cornwall, Devonshire & Somerset . Worthing: the author, 1975.

For effigies, see:

FRYER, Alfred C. 'Monumental effigies in Somerset', S.A.N.H.S., 61(2), 1915, p;.11-30; 62(2), 1916, p.46-85; 63(2), 1917, p.1-20; 64(2), 1918, p.29-45; 65(2), 1919, p.28-47; 66(2), 1920, p.26-55; 67(2), 1921, p.12-38; 68(2), 1922, p.27-63; 69(2), 1923, p.6-29; 70(2), 1924, p.45-85; 71(2), 1925, p.38-56; 72(2), 1926, p.23-45; 74, 1928, p.10-56 See also supplements in 75, 1929, p.34-41 & 76, 1930, p.28-38.

See also:

FRYER, A. C. Index to papers in the Proceedings of the Somersetshire Archaeological and Natural History Society on monumental effigies in Somerset. Taunton: Barnicott & Pearce for the Society, 1932.

A chapter on the heraldic glass of Somerset in included in:

WOODFORDE, Christopher. Stained glass in Somerset, 1250-1830. London: Oxford University press, 1946. Reprinted Bath: Kingsmead Press, 1946.

Brief descriptions of monuments in many East Somerset churches are provided by:

ROBINSON, W. J. West country churches. 4 vols. Bristol: Bristol Times & Mirror, 1914-16. [Covers East Somerset, Bristol, Gloucestershire & Wiltshire]

Inscriptions from a number of churches have been published, and are listed here. It should be remembered that these works are not necessarily comprehensive.

AXBRIDGE

WADE, E. F. 'Monumental inscriptions, with notes, from the church and churchyard of Axbridge, Co. Somerset', M.G.H., N.S., 3, 1880, p.202-4, 310-3, & 381-3.

BATH

'Monumental and other inscriptions of persons of baronets' families in the Abbey Church of Saint Peter and Saint Paul in the city of Bath', Family history, 5(30/31), N.S., 6/7, 1968, p.210-21.

BOYD, S. A. 'Bath Abbey tablets', Somerset Archaeological & Natural History Society. Proceedings of the Bath & District Branch, 1934-8, p.54-60 & 124-8.

GODWIN, J. G. 'Monumental inscriptions in Bath', M.G.H., N.S., 4, 1884, p.30-3, 57-9, 69-71, 82-4, 95-6, 106-8, 110-12, & 146-7. [Includes parish register extracts]

BERKLEY

S., A. 'Monumental inscriptions of Berkley, Co. Somerset', M.G.H., N.S., 4, 1884, p.157.

BICKNOLLER

MARSHALL, George W. 'Monumental inscriptions from Bicknoller, Co. Somerset', Reliquary, 14, 1873-4, p.235-6.

CURRY MALLETT

WIGFIELD, W. Macdonald. 'Curry Mallet church monuments', N.Q.S.D., 30, 1974-80, p.145-6. See also p.257-8.

CURRY RIVEL

SAUNDERS, G. W. 'The North Chapel of St. Andrews church, Curry Rivel, with notes on the heraldry of the chancel, and the will of John de Urtiaco, 1340, by E. H. Bates', S.A.N.H.S., 61(2), 1915, p.31-53. [Includes monumental inscriptions]

EAST QUANTOXHEAD

See Sampford Brett

ILCHESTER

COX, J. S., ed. Transcripts of the tombstones and mural ornaments in the church of St. Mary Major, Ilchester. Ilchester & district occasional papers, 12,. St. Peter Port: Toucan Press, 1979.

ILMINSTER

'Ilminster', G.T., 12(2), 1987, p.65. [Surnames from monumental inscriptions]

KELSTON

'The principal monumental inscriptions in the church and churchyard of Kelston, Somerset', M.G.H., N.S., 3, 1880, p.130-2, 139-40, & 149-51.

LANGPORT

WERE, F. 'Langport church heraldry', N.Q.S.D., 6, 1899, p.196-7. See also p.299-302.

MONTACUTE

BATES, Cadwallader John. 'The armorial glass in the windows of Montacute House', S.A.N.H.S., 32(2), 1886, p.90-111.

NORTH PETHERTON

OLIVER, G. 'North Petherton church, Somersetshire', Notes & gleanings ... Devon & Cornwall, 5, 1892, p.175-6. [Primarily a discussion of monumental inscriptions]

NUNNEY

WERE, F. 'Heraldry of tombs in Nunney church', N.Q.S.D., 7, 1901, p.154-6.

PORLOCK

HALLIDAY, Maria. A description of the monuments and effigies in Porlock Church, Somerset, with reasons deduced from the documents pertaining to the manor and chantry of Porlock for attributing the tomb to the memory of John, fourth Baron Harington, of Aldingham and Elizabeth (Courtenay) his wife ... Torquay: Torquay Directory Co., 1882.

ROAD

S., A. 'The monumental inscriptions at Road, Co. Somerset', Genealogist, 5, 1881, p.153-6.

RUNNINGTON

SHELL, F. S. 'The monumental inscriptions in the church-yard of Runnington, Somerset', M.G.H., 2nd series, 2, 1888, p.7-8.

SAMPFORD BRETT

'Monumental inscriptions at Sampford-Brett and East Quantoxhead, Co. Somerset', Genealogist, 1, 1877, p.29-32.

SELWORTHY

HANCOCK, F. 'Notes on the parish of Selworthy. 1. The church', N.Q.S.D., 3, 1893, p.201-5, 269-71, & 330-2. [Includes monumental inscriptions]

SOUTH PETHERTON

NORRIS, H. 'Monumental and other inscriptions in South Petherton church', N.Q.S.D., 2, 1891, p.169-70, 229-33, & 283-6; 3, 1893, p.31-4, 65-9, 98-9, & 250-5. [Includes parish register extracts]

TAUNTON

COTTLE, James. Some account of the church of St. Mary Magdalene, Taunton, and the restoration thereof. London: Vizetely Bros., 1845. [Includes some inscriptions]

WELLS

JEWERS, A. J. Wells Cathedral: its monumental inscriptions and heraldry, together with the heraldry of the palace, deanery, and vicars close, with annotations from wills, registers, etc., and illustrations of arms. London: Mitchell & Hughes, 1892.

JEWERS, Arthur J. 'Heraldry of Wells Cathedral', N.Q.S.D., 5, 1897-8, p.27-9.

PEREIRA, H. W. 'Brief notes on the heraldry of the glass and other memorials in Wells Cathedral', S.A.N.H.S., 34(2), 1888, p.40-53.

WINCANTON

SWEETMAN, George. Memorials of Wincanton people ... Wincanton: the author, 1896.

WITHAM FRIARY

S., A. 'The monumental inscriptions of Witham Friary church, Co. Somerset', M.G.H., N.S., 4, 1884, p.302.

WRITHLINGTON

BLACKER, B. H. 'Notes on Writhlington parish, Somerset', Western antiquary, 6(12), 1887, p.291-3. [Includes monumental inscriptions, parish register extracts, etc]

--/--

A number of individual monumental inscriptions have been separately published:

BOTREAUX

PAUL, Roland. 'Incised slab, Aller church', S.A.N.H.S., 71, 1925, p.117. [To Reginald Botreaux, 1420]

COLLINS

'Memorial tablets to intruded ministers', N.Q.S.D., 1, 1890, p.231-2. [Monumental inscriptions for Benjamin Collins of Norton sub Hamden, 1662, & Thomas Long of Pendomer, 1658]1

CROYDEN

GODDARD, W. C. G. 'Inscriptions in Christ Church Cathedral, Oxford', N.Q.S.D., 10, 1907, p.227-8. [Elizabeth Swayne of Dorchester, 1634, George Croyden of Wincanton, 1678; William Levett of Bristol, 1693/4]

DAUBENEY

DAUBENY, W. 'The Daubeney family: South Petherton monument', N.Q.S.D., 2, 1891, p.6-8.

HAMLET, J. 'Daubeney tomb at Jerusalem', N.Q.S.D., 5, 1897-8, p.241-6. See also 6, 1899, p.75-6. [13th c.]

SAUNDERS, G. W. 'The effigy of Sir Philip de Albini', N.Q.S.D., 19, 1929, p.217-20. See also p.244-6 & 280. [1285; Daubeney family; includes pedigree, 12-14th c.]

'The Daubeney tomb in South Petherton church', N.Q.S.D., 1, 1890, p.241-3.

'The tomb of Philip D'Aubigny at Jerusalem', N.Q.S.D., 2, 1891, p.31-33. [13th c.]

DELAMERE

SMITH, S. N. 'Delamere and Paulet monuments in the church at Nunney, Somerset', M.G.H., 5th series, 9, 1935-7, p.84-9. [Includes pedigree of Constance Paulet]

GODWIN

EELES, Francis C. 'The monument of Thomas Godwyn, Bishop of Bath and Wells, 1590', N.Q.S.D., 18, 1926, p.198-9. [At Wokingham, Berkshire]

GORE

WERE, F. 'Gore monument in Barrow Gurney church', N.Q.S.D., 7, 1901, p.344-5. [17th c.]

HARDWICK

CURTIS, C. D. 'Congresbury: Hardwick memorial', N.Q.S.D., 28, 1968, p.169-70.

HARINGTON

POYNTON, F. J. 'The monumental inscriptions of the family of Harington, co. Somerset', M.G.H., N.S., 3, 1880, p.33-4, 59-63, & 89-93.

HAWKER

BATES HARBIN, E. H. 'Hawker brass in Yeovil church', N.Q.S.D., 16, 1920, p.44-7. [Thomas Hawker, 1696]

HODGES

P., J. W. D. 'Military brass in Wedmore church, Somerset', N.Q.S.D., 20, 1930-32, p.226-7. [Thomas Hodges, 1583]

HUNGERFORD

ROGERS, W. H. H. 'The "heart-case" and tomb of Sir Edward Hungerford, ob. 1648, at Farleigh-Hungerford, Somerset', N.Q.S.D., 7, 1901, p.10-13. See also p.64-5.

IRESON

GRAY, H. St. George. 'Nathaniel Ireson of Wincanton, master builder', S.A.N.H.S., 87. 1941, p.81-4. [Includes inscriptions of Ireson and Morrish]

JENYNS

WERE, F. 'The heraldry of the Jenyns brass, Churchill, Somerset', Proceedings of the Clifton Antiquarian Club, 4, 1900, p.71-2.

MIDDLETON

ROBINSON, J. Armitage. 'The effigy of 'John de Middleton' at Wells', S.A.N.H.S., 71(2), 1925, p.77-87.

MORRISH

See Ireson

NASH

DAMER POWELL, J. 'Nash family of Wells', N.Q.S.D., 20, 1932, p.272. [Monumental inscription to Ann Nash, 1777]

NORTON

WERE, Francis. 'Heraldry on the tomb of the Nortons in Abbotsleigh church', S.A.N.H.S., 68(2), 1922, p.105-7. [Medieval]

PALMER

CURTIS, C. D. 'The last survivor of the Battle of Corunna', N.Q.S.D., 28, 1968, p.197-8. [Monumental inscription to Thomas Palmer, 1889, at Weston-Super-Mare]

PENNE

GERRARD, A. W. 'The Penne brass in Yeovil church', N.Q.S.D., 16, 1920, p.215-6. See also p.259.

ROGERS, W. H. H. 'The Penne brass, Yeovil church', N.Q.S.D., 9, 1905, p.105-7. See also p.154-5 & 202-3.

PITT

NEVILL, Edm. 'Pitt family from Ilminster, Somerset', N.Q.S.D., 11, 1909, p.332. [Memorial inscriptions from Wimbledon, Surrey, 17-19th c.]

POWLETT

FRYER, Alfred C. 'Notes on the effigies of Sir John Poulet and Constance, his wife, in the church of All Saints, Nunney', S.A.N.H.S., 80(2), 1934, p.120-23.

ROGERS, W. H. H. 'The Powlett brass, Minety Church, Wilts', N.Q.S.D., 6, 1899, p.193-6.

'Monumental inscriptions', S.A.N.H.S., 17, 1871, p.70-72. [Sir Amias Poulet of Hinton, 1588]

ROSE

S., A. J. P. 'Southleigh church, Co. Devon', N.Q.S.D., 10, 1907, p.279-80. See also p.306-7. [Monumental inscription to Sir John Rose of Winsham, Somerset, 1705, with will of Richard Rose of Watton Fitzpaine, Dorset, 1657]

SPEKE

R., W. H. H. 'The Speke brass, Dowlish-Wake church, Somerset', N.Q.S.D., 30, 10, 1907, p.1-2. [1528]

STAWELL

STAWELL, G. D. 'Notes on the Stawell monuments in Cothelstone church', N.Q.S.D., 11, 1909, p.193-5. See also p.281-2.

SYDENHAM

S., A. J. P. 'Broadhembury church, Co. Devon', N.Q.S.D., 10, 1907, p.275. [Monumental inscriptions to Ellen Sydenham of Combe, Somerset, 1794, & Richard Hill of Priory, 1737]

TRENCHARD

B., S. R. 'John Trenchard of Evershot', N.Q.S.D., 4, 1894-5, p.365. [Monumental inscription]

VENN

'Venn family of Lydeard St. Lawrence, Somerset', N.Q.S.D., 90, 1905, p.73-4. [Monumental inscription]

WILSON

TORRENS, H. S. 'A monumental inscription from the Countess of Huntingdon's Chapel, Bath', N.Q.S.D., 32, 1986-, p.675-7. [Monumental inscription to Elizabeth Wilson, nee Lloyd, 1820]

WYER

DANIEL, W. E. 'Memorial to an ejected minister: Dositheus Wyer, Cloford', N.Q.S.D., 1, 1890, p.265-6. [Includes genealogical notes]

WYNDHAM

D'ELBOUX, R. H. 'Nicholas Stone's monument to Sir John Wyndham, at St. Decuman's, Watchet', S.A.N.H.S., 92, 1946, p.88-92.

There are many inscriptions relating to Dorset men and women in other counties. For these, see:

'Monumental inscriptions in other counties relating to Somerset and Dorset', N.Q.S.D, 3, 1893, p.337-8; 4, 1895-5, p.123, 160, 218, 310, & 373; 5, 1897-8, p.131, 187, 312, & 356; 6, 1899, p.93-4, 163-4, & 231; 7, 1901, p.72-5, 98-102, 156-9, 208-10, 274-81; 8, 1903, p.44-8, 78-80, 124-7, & 261-5; 9, 1905, p.361-3; 9, 1905, p.90-93 & 132-5; 9, 1905, p.189-92; 10, 1907, p.359-61; 11, 1909, p.82-6, 129-31 & 273-7; 12, 1911, p.37-8, 82-3, 183, & 229-32; 13, 1913, p.36, 83-6, 132-5, & 275-6; 14, 1915, p.133-5; 15, 1917, p.140-2; 17, 1923, p.218. 20, 1930-32, p.254-5; 21, 1935, p.278.

BAKER, T. H. 'Somerset and Dorset inscriptions in Salisbury Cathedral', N.Q.S.D., 10, 1907, p.127-30, 179-80, & 229-30.

GODDARD, W. C. G. 'Inscriptions in Christ Church Cathedral, Oxford', N.Q.S.D., 10, 1907, p.227-8. [Dorset and Somerset memorials]

WILLIAMS, H. F. Fulford. 'Somerset and Dorset monumental inscriptions in the British cemetery at Lisbon', N.Q.S.D., 24, 1946, p.279-84.

R. 'Somerset and Dorset inscriptions on tombs in Bunhill fields', N.Q.S.D., 5, 1897-8, p.356-7. [Includes monumental inscription to Richard Fairclough, rector of Mells, & son of Samuel Fairclough of Suffolk]

WAINWRIGHT, Thos. 'Somerset and Dorset inscriptions in Devon', N.Q.S.D., 9, 1905, p.235-8 & 275-9.

R. 'Somerset inscriptions in Hants', N.Q.S.D., 6, 1899, p.275-6. [Helyar, Wyndham, Cheese, and Pendilton inscriptions]

BAKER, T. H. 'Fisherton Anger register, Wilts: Somerset and Dorset marriages', N.Q.S.D., 11, 1909, p.277-81.

CHAPTER 11
OFFICIAL LISTS OF NAMES

Governments are keen on listing their subjects, much to the disgust of folk like Wat Tyler. Lists are made for many reasons - taxation, defence, voting, land ownership, etc. These lists are invaluable sources of information for the genealogist; they enable ancestors to be precisely located in time and place. The earliest such list for Somerset is printed in:

THORN, Caroline & Frank, eds. Domesday book, 8: Somerset. Chichester: Phillimore, 1980.

A number of works include early tax lists:

DICKINSON, F. H., ed. Kirby's quest for Somerset. Nomina villarum for Somerset of 16th of Edward the 3rd. Exchequer lay subsidies 169/5, which is a tax roll for Somerset of the first year of Edward the 3rd. County rate of 1742. Hundreds and parishes etc of Somerset as given in the census of 1841. Somerset Record Society, 3. Bath: the Society, 1889.

Inquisitions and assessments relating to feudal aids; with other analogous documents preserved in the Public Record Office. Vol. 4: Northampton-Somerset. London: H.M.S.O., 1906.

MONDAY, A. J. 'Knight service in the county of Somerset in the time of Henry II', Western antiquary, 6(6-8), 1886-7, p.147-9 & 185-8.

Bath subsidies are transcribed in:

GREEN, E. 'A Bath poll tax 2 Richard II', Proceedings of the Bath Natural History & Antiquarian Field Club, 6, 1889, p.294-315.

GREEN, Emanuel. 'Bath lay subsidies, Henry IV to Henry VIII', Proceedings of the Bath Natural History & Antiquarian Field Club, 6, 1889, p.379-411.

The Wiveliscombe portion of the 1327 lay subsidy is in:

'Lay subsidy, 1327', G.T., 13(1), 1988, p.21.

SHICKLE, C. W. 'On the subsidy roll of Somerset in the 13th year of Henry IV', Proceedings of the Bath Natural History and Antiquarian Field Club, 9, 1901, p.188-201.

A number of late sixteenth century muster rolls, etc., are printed in:

GREEN, Emanuel. The preparation in Somerset against the Spanish Armada, A.D. 1558-1588. London: Harrison & Sons, 1888.

Contributors to Armada expenses, with some genealogical notes, are listed in:

'Armada expenses in Somerset and Dorset, A.D. 1589', N.Q.S.D., 1, 1890, p.33-40.

Notes on musters in the early seventeenth century are included amongst the lieutenancy papers of the Earl of Hertford, Lord Lieutenant of Somerset, as well as of Wiltshire & Bristol. See:

MURPHY, W. P. D., ed. The Earl of Hertford's lieutenancy papers, 1603-1612. Wiltshire Record Society, 23. Devizes: the Society, 1969.

Many other lists of names are available for seventeenth-century Somerset. The lay subsidy returns are given in:

DWELLY, E., ed. XVII century directory of Somerset, containing the names of all persons paying taxes or exempted from payment, copied from the original lay subsidy rolls in the Record Office. Dwelly's national records, 2(in 5 pts). Fleet, Hants: E. Dwelly, 1929-32. [This was incomplete until the appearance of Stoate's Dwelly's index. (see below)]

In 1641, as civil war loomed, Parliament required every subject to take an oath of loyalty. The consequent 'protestation' returns are printed in:

STOATE, T. L., ed. The Somerset protestation returns and lay subsidy rolls, 1641/2, transcribed by A.J. Howard. Bristol: the editor, 1975.

A number of other minor civil war lists may be found in:

SYMONDS, Henry. 'A by-path of the Civil War', S.A.N.H.S., 65(2), 1919, p.48-75. [Lists inhabitants of South Brent, Berrow, Burnham, & Lympsham, who were plundered; also includes certificates subscribed by many inhabitants of East Brent, Burnham, Berrow, & South Brent, 1645]

A 'free and voluntary present' was requested by the restored Charles II in 1661; for the Chewton Hundred return, see:

HOLMYARD, E. J. 'Lay subsidy roll, Chewton Hundred, 1661', N.Q.S.D., 14, 1915, p.54-6.

The insufficiency of the subsidy led to the imposition of the hearth tax in the later seventeenth century. See:

HOLWORTHY, R., ed. Hearth tax for Somerset 1664-5, with indices, copied from the original rolls in the Public Record Office. Dwelly's national records, 1. Fleet, Hants: E. Dwelly, 1916. [See also STOATE, T. L., ed. Dwelly's index to the Somerset hearth tax exemption certificates of 1670 and 1674, with a completion of part 5 of Dwelly's 'National records', vol. 2. Bristol: the editor, 1976

GREEN, Emanuel. 'A benevolence granted to Charles II by the hundreds of Williton, Freemanors and Carhampton', S.A.N.H.S., 35(2), 1889, p.53-82.

In the eighteenth and early nineteenth centuries, voting was not secret, and poll books giving the names of electors and how they cast their votes were published after elections. Many Somerset poll books survive; one has recently been reprinted as:

The Bath poll book, 1855. Milton Keynes: Open University Press, 1974.

Most surviving poll books relate to the boroughs of the county. Only a handful of copies survive for any single poll - if you are lucky. Manuscript poll books are also available. Surviving poll books are listed in the works identified in the companion volume to the present work, English genealogy: an introductory bibliography. It is unlikely that they would be available for loan from any of the libraries which hold them, so full bibliographic details are not given here. Poll books are available for the boroughs and elections listed below:

BATH

1835, 1837, 1841, 1847, 1851, 1855, 1857, 1859, 1868.

BRIDGWATER

1754, 1780, 1802, 1806, 1807, 1818, 1826, 1831, 1835, 1837, 1841, 1847, 1852, 1857, 1865, 1866.

TAUNTON

1853.

WELLS

1765.

A list of candidates in Ilchester elections, with votes cast, is given in:

WELBY, Alfred 'Ilchester Parliamentary elections, 1802-1831', N.Q.S.D. , 20, 1932, p.248-9.

The most useful lists deriving from official activity are the census enumerators returns of the nineteenth century. Surnames appearing in the 1851 census are indexed in:

1851 census surname index. 7 vols. Taunton: Somerset & Dorset Family History Society, 1985- [v.1. West Somerset. v.2, Taunton. v.3. Bridgwater Langport & Ilminster. v.4. Yeovil area. v.5. Wincanton-Frome area. v.6. Wells, Shepton Mallet area. ---]

See also:

'Jolly Jack Tar', G.T., 12(2), 1987, p.63. [Somerset & Dorset sailors in Edinburgh during the 1851 census]

Surnames from the 1881 census for South Cadbury are listed in:

MILLER, S. W. 'South Cadbury', G.T., 12(3), 1987, p.90.

The problems posed by enumerators' use of initials are discussed in:

McCALL, R. 'Initials', G.T., 13(2), 1988, p.43.

CHAPTER 12
DIRECTORIES, GAZETTEERS AND MAPS

Directories are an invaluable source of information about people in the past. For the nineteenth century, they are the equivalent of the modern phone book. Many directories for Somerset were published; I have endeavoured to identify all those published in the nineteenth century and earlier which include information of genealogical value. Selected directories for the twentieth century are also included in the following list, which is arranged chronologically and by place. Directories covering a large number of counties are not included here; they may be identified by consulting the sources listed in the companion volume to the present work, English genealogy: an introductory bibliography.

TUNNICLIFF, William. A topographical survey of the counties of Somerset, Gloucester, Worcester, Stafford, Cheshire and Lancaster. London: R. Cruttwell, 1789.

WELBY, Alfred. 'Glastonbury, Somerton, Wrington, in 1792', N.Q.S.D., 21, 1932, p.27-30. [From the Universal British Directory]

A general directory for the county of Somerset. Taunton: William Bragg, 1840. [Only gives names for the towns]

Hunt & Co's Directory and Topography of the Towns of Axbridge, Burnham, Bruton, Castle Cary, ... Weston-super-Mare, Wincanton and Yeovil (including Bristol). London: Hunt, E. & Co. 1850.

Slater's royal national and commercial directory and topography of the counties of Cornwall, Devonshire, Dorsetshire and Somersetshire. Manchester: I. Slater, 1852-3.

Harrison, Harrod & Co's Bristol post office directory and gazetteer with the counties of Gloucester & Somersetshire. London: Harrison & Harrod, 1859.

Kelly's Directory of Somersetshire. London: Kelly & Co. 1861-1939. [17 eds.]

Post Office Directory of Somerset and Bristol. London: Kelly & Co. 1861-1883. [3 eds.]

Smith & Co's Bath & Somerset Directory. London: Smith & Co. 1865.

Post Office directory of Somerset & Devon with Bristol. London: Kelly & Co., 1866.

Morris & Co's commercial directory and gazetteer of Somersetshire with Bristol. 2 vols. Nottingham: Morris & Co., 1872.

W. E. Owen & Co's general, topographical and historical directory for the counties of Wiltshire, Somersetshire with the cities of Bristol and Bath. Leicester: W. E. Owen & Co., 1878.

W. E. Owen & Co's general, topographical and historical directory for Gloucester-shire, Wiltshire, Somerset-shire, Monmouthshire, Radnorshire, with the cities of Bristol and Bath. Leicester: W. E. Owen & Co., 1879.

Kelly's directory of Somersetshire & Gloucestershire with the city of Bristol. London: Kelly & Co., 1889-1939. [13 eds.]

Somersetshire, Dorsetshire and Wiltshire directory. Walsall: Aubrey & Co., 1909-41. [6 eds.]

Kelly's directory of the counties of Somerset and Gloucester, with the city of Bristol. London: Kellys Directories, 1927.

Bath Annual Directory. Bath: C. Clark. 1850.

A Directory for the City & Borough of Bath and the City of Wells. Bath: S. Vivian, 1852-4. [2 eds.]

The Bath Directory. Bath: R. E. Peach, 1856

Post Office Bath Directory. Bath: W. Lewis. 1858-1940. [20 eds.]

Kelly's Directory of Bath & Neighbourhood. London: Kelly's Directories Ltd. 1904-1950. [4 eds.]

John Whitby & Son's Handy Directory of Bridgwater and Neighbourhood. Bridgwater: Whitby, J. & Son. 1883-97. [2 eds.]

E. T. Page's Directory of Bridgwater and neighbourhood. Bridgwater: Page, E. T. 1890.

Bridgwater Directory and Guide, including fifty villages. Bridgwater: Whitby, J. & Sons Ltd. 1908.

COX, J. Stevens, ed. An Ilchester directory of 1840. Ilchester and District occasional papers, 5. St. Peter Port: Toucan Press, 1972. [Reprint of Ilchester section of Bragg's directory]

Frome Almanack and Directory and Chamber of Commerce Guide. Frome: Harvey & Woodland. 1916-1931. [2 eds.]

ADAMS, SAMPSON & CO. Taunton directory, containing the names of the citizens and town officers, a business directory, general events of the years 1856 and 1857, and an almanac for 1859. Taunton: Samuel G. Dunbar, 1859.

Goodmans's Directory of Taunton and its neighbourhood. Taunton: Goodman, E. 1864.

Goodman and Son's Illustrated Guide and Directory of Taunton. Taunton: Goodman & Son. 1887-1906. [5 eds.]

Kelly's Directory of Taunton. London: Kelly's Directories Ltd. 1928-1948. [10 eds.]

The Wellington and Wiveliscombe Directory. Wellington: I. Tozer, 1912-1933. [2 eds.]

J. Wright & Co's Weston-Super-Mare & Clevedon Directory. Bristol: J. Wright, 1880-1891. [4 eds.]

Collins' History of Yeovil and Directory. Yeovil: Beale Collins, W. 1905, 1907.

Yeovil, Sherborne & District Directory. Yeovil: Snell, E. 1927-1949. [7 eds.]

Directories sometimes, usefully, include maps, which you will need to consult in order to identify particular places. If you can get hold of an early map, you will be able to see how far the landscape has changed since its compilation. A number have been recently reprinted:

The old series Ordnance Survey maps of England and Wales, vol. VI: Devon, Cornwall and West Somerset. Lympne Castle: Harry Margary, 1977.

HARLEY, J. B., & DUNNING, R. W., eds. Somerset maps: Day and Masters, 1782; Greenwood, 1822. Somerset Record Society, 76. Taunton: the Society, 1981.

Many others are listed in:

CHUBB, Thomas. A descriptive list of the printed maps of Somersetshire, 1575-1914. Taunton: Somersetshire Archaeological & Natural History Society, 1914.

Manuscript maps for northern Somerset, including tithe, enclosure, and estate maps, are listed in:

A catalogue of historic maps in Avon. Bristol: County of Avon, [1984].

CHAPTER 13
RELIGIOUS RECORDS

The church formerly played a much greater role in society than it does today. Consequently, many of the sources essential to the genealogist are to be found in ecclesiastical rather than state archives - for example, parish registers, probate records, local government records, etc. Works on ecclesiastical sources may be found throughout this bibliography; this chapter concentrates on those topics which are primarily to do with diocesan administration - mainly bishops' registers, and lists of clergy.

The Church of England clergy in Somerset from the 13th century to 1738 are listed in:

WEAVER, Frederick William. Somerset incumbents, from the Hugo mss. 30,279-80 in the British Museum. Bristol: C.T.Jefferies & Sons for the editor, 1889.

See also:

LYTE, Sir H. C. Maxwell. 'Somerset incumbents, A.D. 1354-1401', S.A.N.H.S., 78, 1932, p.44-108.

COLEMAN, Prebendary. 'The prebend and prebendaries of Warminster, alias Lurvile, in the Cathedral church of Wells', S.A.N.H.S., 47(2), 1901, p.189-216.

MEADE, Canon. 'Historical notes on the church of Castle Cary', S.A.N.H.S., 16(2), 1870, p.1-12. [Includes list of vicars, 14-19th c.]

POYNTON, F. J. 'Names of the rectors of Kelston, Co. Somerset, of the patrons who presented them, and of the bishops who gave them institution , from the year 1325 to the present time, 1876', M.G.H., N.S., 2, 1877, p.333-5, 350-2, 360-3, 379-81, 407-10, 428-31, 460, 477-8, 501-2, 525-7, & 549-51.

Lists of clergy covering shorter periods are noted in the appropriate section below.

A. The Pre-Reformation Church

Bishops registers in the medieval period constituted the principal records of diocesan administration. They include lists of institutions and ordinations, records of estate administration, records of cases heard before the ecclesiastical courts, records of probate, and much else of interest to the genealogist. Most medieval bishops' registers for Somerset have been published:

HOBHOUSE, Edmund, ed. Calendar of the register of John de Drokensford, bishop of Bath and Wells, A.D. 1309-1329. Somerset Record Society, 1. [ ]: the Society, 1887.

HOLMES, Thomas Scott, ed. The register of Ralph of Shrewsbury, bishop of Bath and Wells, 1329-1363. Somerset Record Society, 9-10. Taunton: the Society, 1896.

HOLMES, Thomas Scott, ed. The registers of Walter Giffard, bishop of Bath and Wells, 1265-6, and of Henry Bowett, bishop of Bath and Wells, 1401-7. Somerset Record Society, 13. Taunton: the Society, 1899.

HOLMES, Thomas Scott, ed. The register of Nicholas Bubwith,bishop of Bath and Wells, 1407-1424. Somerset Record Society, 29-30. Taunton: the Society, 1914-1915.

HOLMES, Thomas Scott, ed. The register of John Stafford, bishop of Bath and Wells, 1425-1443. Somerset Record Society, 31-2. Taunton: the Society, 1915-1916. [This volume is corrected in: JONES, I. Fitzroy. 'Bishop Stafford's register', N.Q.S.D., 23, 1942, p.117-8 & 126-9.]

MAXWELL-LYTE, Sir H. C., & DAWES, M. C. B., eds. The register of Thomas Bekynton, bishop of Bath and Wells, 1443-1465. Somerset Record Society, 49-50. Taunton: the Society, 1934-1935.

LYTE, Sir H. C. Maxwell, ed. The registers of Robert Stillington, bishop of Bath and Wells, 1466-1491, and Richard Fox, bishop of Bath and Wells, 1492-1494. Somerset Record Society, 52. [Taunton]: the Society, 1937. [This volume excludes ordination lists, which have, however, been included in an earlier edition of Bishop Fox's register: BATTEN, Edmund Chisholm, ed. The register of Richard Fox, while Bishop of Bath and Wells, A. D. MCCCCXCII-MCCCCXCIV. London: privately printed, 1889]

LYTE, Sir Henry Maxwell, ed. The registers of Oliver King, bishop of Bath and Wells, 1496-1503, and Hadrian de Castello, bishop of Bath and Wells, 1503-1518. Somerset Record Society, 54. Taunton: the Society, 1939.

LYTE, Sir Henry Maxwell, ed. The registers of Thomas Wolsey, bishop of Bath and Wells, 1518-1523, John Clerke, bishop of Bath and Wells, 1523-1541, William Knyght, bishop of Bath and Wells, 1541-1547, and Gilbert Bourne, bishop of Bath and Wells, 1554-1559. Somerset Record Society, 55. Taunton: the Society, 1940.

Similar records are to be found in:

COLCHESTER, L. S. The earliest extant register of the Vicars Choral of Wells (1393-1534). [Wells]: [privately printed], 1985.

DICKINSON, F. H., ed. Indexes to the record books of the Dean and Chapter of the cathedral church of S. Andrew, Wells. Bristol: C. T. Jefferies & Sons, 1876.

These and other sources have been systematically combed in order to compile a comprehensive list of pre-reformation diocesan dignitaries. See:

LE NEVE, John. Fasti ecclesiae Anglicanae, 1300-1541. Vol. 8. Bath and Wells diocese, comp. B. Jones. London: Athlone Press, University of London, 1964. See also vol.12 for errata and indexes of persons and places.

Early Somerset archdeacons, and deans of Wells, are identified in:

ROBINSON, J. Armitage. Somerset historical essays. London: Oxford University Press for the British Academy, 1921.

Other clergy are listed in a number of works:

D., L. L. 'Somerset institutions', N.Q.S.D., 5, 1897-8, p.145-7. See also 17, 1923, p.159. [By the Chapter of Canterbury Cathedral, during 1503 vacancy of the See]

FRY, E. A. 'Early references to clergy in Dorset and Somerset', N.Q.S.D., 17, 1923, p.271-6; 18, 1926, p.64-8, 203-6, & 241-8; 19, 1929, p.128-31 & 159-63; 20, 1030-32, p.35-6, 112-5, 133-5 & 178-9. [Clergy not mentioned in the bishops' registers; this list was not completed]

DUNNING, Robert W. 'Somerset parochial clergy, 1373-1404', S.A.N.H.S., 114, 1969-70, p.91-5. [List]

Monastic records provide many names of monks:

WEAVER, F. W. 'The fate of the dispossessed monks and nuns', S.A.N.H.S., 38(2), 1892, p.327-46. [Includes many names. See also: BASKERVILLE, G. 'Dispossessed abbots', N.Q.S.D., 21, 1935, p. 137-8.]

W[EAVER], F. W. 'The Priory of Burtle alias Spraulesmede', N.Q.S.D., 4, 1894-5, p.249-50. [Includes list of priors]

KEIL, Ian. 'The succession of the abbots of Glastonbury, 1274-1342', N.Q.S.D., 27, 1961, p.216-8.

GASQUET, F. A. 'A list of Glastonbury monks and others of their household in A.D. 1377', Downside review, 11, 1892, p.150-51.

'Witham Friary', N.Q.S.D., 2, 1891, p.206-7. [List of monks pensioned off at the Dissolution]

Monastic records also provide the names of many laymen. Recipients of corrodies - that is, monetary allowances - from Glastonbury Abbey are listed in:

KEIL, Ian. 'Corrodies of Glastonbury Abbey in the later middle ages', S.A.N.H.S., 108, 1963/4, p.113-31.

On the dissolution of the monasteries, see:

BETTEY, J. H. The Suppression of the monasteries in the West of England. Gloucester: Alan Sutton, 1989.

Another useful works on the medieval church include:

CHURCH, C. M. Chapters in the early history of the church of Wells, A.D. 1136-1333 from documents in possession of the Dean and Chapter. London: Elliot Stock, 1894. [Includes pedigrees of Bishops Reginald, 1174-91, and Savaric, 1192-1205, and abstracts of many deeds]

B. The Church of England

Post-Reformation bishops' registers have not so far been edited. See, however:

JENKINS, Claude, ed. 'Act book of the archdeacon of Taunton', in Palmer, T. F., ed. Collectanea II. Somerset Record Society, 43. Taunton: the Society, 1928.

COLCHESTER, L. S. Act book, 1541-1593, of the Vicars Choral of Wells. [Wells]: privately printed], 1986.

BAILEY, Derrick Sherwin, ed. Wells Cathedral chapter act book, 1666-1683. Somerset Record Society, 73. Taunton: the Society, 1973.

Diocesan dignitaries are listed in:

LE NEVE, J. Fasti ecclesiae Anglicanae, 1541-1857, v.5: Bath & Wells Diocese, comp. Joyce M. Horn & Derrick Sherwin Bailey. London: Institute of Historical Research, 1979.

A detailed study of the diocese of Bath and Wells in the early seventeenth century, including a list of clergy, is provided by:

STIEG, Margaret. Laud's laboratory: the Diocese of Bath and Wells in the early seventeenth century. Lewisburg: Bucknold University press, 1982.

A number of other general lists of clergy are available in print:

JONES, I. Fitzroy. 'Deprived incumbents in Somerset, 1554-6', N.Q.S.D., 24, 1946, p.199-203.

FAIRBROTHER, E. H. 'Somerset clergy, tempore Elizabethae', N.Q.S.D., 13, 1913, p.269-71 & 332-5; 14, 1915, p.31-3, 63-5, 105-7, 170-1, 206-8, 265-8, 305-6, & 329-32; 15, 1917, p.13-14, 95-7, 114-6, 161-5, & 203-4.

FRY, E. A. 'Dispensations to hold livings in plurality, 1559-1569', N.Q.S.D., 13, 1913, p.73-8. [In Somerset & Dorset]

THOMPSON, E. Margaret. 'Ministers in Somerset during the Commonwealth', N.Q.S.D., 13, 1913, p.156-60. [List of those 'intruded' during the Interregnum]

HELLIER, E. Joseph D. 'Somerset non-jurors', N.Q.S.D., 17, 1923, p.182-3. See also p.82 & 147. [List of clergy in 1689]

'Somerset incumbents ordained at Gloucester, 1684-9', N.Q.S.D., 25, 1950, p.213-4.

Occupants of the Close at Wells are traced in:

BAILEY, Derrick Sherwin. Canonical houses of Wells. Gloucester: Alan Sutton, 1982.

The names of many clergy in the Archdeaconry of Wells are given in:

'Address of sympathy to Irish clergy from the Archdeacon and clergy of the Archdeaconry of Wells, July 1836', N.Q.S.D., 21, 1935, p.111-4. [Includes names of many clergy in the Archdeaconry]

Pastores redivivi, or, brief memorials of ministers who officiated in the parish churches of Wincanton, Bruton, Stoke Trister, Templecombe, Upton Noble, Milborne Port, and North Cadbury, in the 17th century. Wincanton: John Davis, 1841.

Innumerable histories of particular churches have been compiled, and frequently include clergy lists, inscriptions, parish register extracts, etc. These cannot be listed here; you should ask one of the libraries listed above what is available. Lists of clergy in particular churches, together with other miscellaneous printed sources, are to be found in:

BATH

HENNING, G. S. 'Rectors of Bath', N.Q.S.D., 5, 1897-8, p.81.

BEDMINSTER

TAYLOR, C. S. 'The early history of the Bedminster churches', Proceedings of the Clifton Antiquarian Club, 2, 1893, p.179-213. [Includes list of clergy]

CHEWTON

JONES, I. Fitzroy. 'Lecturers at Chewton (c.1628-32)', N.Q.S.D., 24. 1946, p.136. [List of clergy]

EAST LYDFORD

HENNING, G. S. 'Rectors of East Lydford', N.Q.S.D., 5, 1897-8, p.30-1. [List 1745-1895]

HIGH HAM

HAYWARD, Douglas L. 'Apportionment of seats in Low Ham church', N.Q.S.D., 4, 1894-5, p.167-8. [Seating plan, 1699; this church is in the parish of High Ham]

REDCLIFFE

WILLIAMS, E. E. The chantries of Wiliam Canynges in St. Mary, Redcliffe, Bristol. Bristol: Wm. George's Sons, 1950. [Includes accounts, 1475-1545, and notes on the Canynges family]

THURLOXTON

BARTLETT, R. G. 'Rectors of Thurloxton, Somerset', N.Q.S.D., 4, 1894-5, p.366. [List, 1558-1859]

WELLS

CHURCH, C. M. 'The prebendaries of Wells Cathedral Church, 1551', N.Q.S.D., 6, 1999, p.321-2, & 7, 1901, p.129-31. [List]

WATKIN, Aelred, ed. 'The precentors, chancellors and treasurers in Wells Cathedral', in PALMER, T. F., ed. Collectanea III: a collection of documents from various sources. Somerset Record Society, 57. Taunton: the Society, 1942.

WINSFORD

SEAMAN, Charles E. 'Vicars of Winsford, Somerset', N.Q.S.D., 4, 1894-5, p.264-5. [List, 1664-1857]

C. Roman Catholics

Many notes on Roman Catholic families, together with a biographical dictionary of missionaries in the South-West, are in:

OLIVER, George. Collections illustrating the history of the Catholic religion in Devonshire, Cornwall, Dorset, Somerset and Wilts. London: Keating & Brown, 1826.

T., E. M. 'A list of Somerset recusants, 34 Eliz. - 3 James I', N.Q.S.D., 5, 1897-8, p.112-6.

WILLIAMS, J. Anthony, ed. Post-Reformation Catholicism in Bath, 1559-1850. Catholic Record Society publications (record series), 65-6. London: the Society, 1975-6. [Includes register, 1780-1825, 1767 return of Papists, list of Papist oaths taken in 1791, will of Francis Carne, 1719-20, etc. etc.]

MEADEN, Linda. 'Shepton Mallett R.C's, 1858 and 1883', G.T., 8(3), 1983, p.80-1. [Names and occupations from church censuses]

TRAPPES-LOMAX, Richard, ed. The English Franciscan nuns, 1619-1821, and the Friars Minor of the same province, 1618-1761. Catholic Record Society publications, 24. London: the Society, 1922. [Includes records of the 19th c. nunnery at Taunton]

D. Nonconformists

The civil war of the mid-seventeenth century spawned many dissenting sects. Clergy ejected from their livings after the restoration of Charles II are listed in:

BELLAMY, J. 'Ejected and silenced', G.T., 13(2), 1988, p.59-61.

Many biographical notes on early Quakers are given in:

MORLAND, Stephen C., ed. The Somersetshire quarterly meeting of the Society of Friends, 1668-1699. Somerset Record Society, 75. Taunton: the Society, 1978.

See also:

MORLAND, S. C. 'A mid-Somerset meeting in the seventeenth century: Long Sutton', Journal of the Friends Historical Society, 55(1 & 2), 1986 (for 1983 & 1984), p.4-24. [Includes list of names with some ages and occupations, 1670 & 1700]

Quakers prosecuted for their faith in the late 17th and early 18th centuries are listed in:

SCHOMBERG, Arthur. 'Quakers in Dorset and Somerset', N.Q.S.D., 5, 1897-8, p.231-3, 262-4, 291-4, & 350-2.

Many histories of non-conformity in Somerset are available, but cannot be listed here. A number of works giving the names of later non-conformists may, however, be cited:

TITFORD, John S. 'Church records: Badcox Lane Baptist, Frome', G.T., 8(2), 1983, p.57. [Includes names of many church members, c.1740]

COSTEN, M. D., ed. Wesleyans and Bible Christians in South Somerset accounts and minutes, 1808-1907. Somerset Record Society, 78. Taunton: the Society, 1984.

CROFTS, Bruce, ed. At Satan's throne: the story of Methodism in Bath over 250 years. Bristol: White Tree Books, 1990. [Includes list of ministers appointed to the Bath Circuit]

WARFIELD, D. A. A lively people: the story of a village Methodist society. Paulton: Purnell & Sons, 1960. [History of Paulton methodists, including lists of ministers and officers]

MURCH, Jerome. A history of the Presbyterian and General Baptist churches in the West of England, with memoirs of some of their pastors. London: R. Hunter, 1835. [Includes lists of ministers in Gloucestershire, Wiltshire, Somerset, Dorset, Devon & Cornwall]

CHAPTER 14
ESTATE AND FAMILY PAPERS

A. GENERAL

The records of estate administration - deeds, leases, rentals, surveys, etc - are a mine of information for the genealogist. Many of these records have been published in part or full - although far more still lie untouched in the archives. A number of deed collections have been published; see:

GREEN, Emanuel, ed. Pedes finium, commonly called feet of fines, for the county of Somerset. Somerset Record Society, 6, 12, 17, & 22. Taunton: the Society, 1892-1906. [1st series: 1196-1307. 2nd series: 1307-46. 3rd series: 1347-1399. 4th series: Henry IV-Henry VI.]

HARBIN, Sophia W. Bates, ed. Somerset enrolled deeds. Somerset Record Society, 51. Taunton: the Society, 1936. [This is supplemented by: HOBBS, S. D. 'Somerset enrolled deeds', N.Q.S.D., 31, 1980-85, p.281-2.]

MONDAY, Alfred James. 'The county records of Somerset: an index to the "head deeds and other documents enrolled" with the custos rotulorum', N.Q.S.D., 1, 1909, p.101-12 & 146-56. [Indexes 471 enrolled deeds, 16-19th c.]

Stray Somerset deeds are listed in a number of works:

FUDGE, W. K. 'The value of old parchment documents in genealogical and topographical research', Topographical quarterly, 3(2), 1935, p.85-108

MEDLYCOTT, Mervyn T. 'Somerset deeds at Bristol University Library', G.T., 10(1), 1984/5, p.55.

'List of Somerset charters and documents in the Bodleian Library, Oxford (XI.35)', N.Q.S.D., 23, 1942, p.321-7. See also p.348.

MEDLYCOTT, Mervyn T. Somerset deeds at the National Library of Wales', G.T., 1(1), 1975, p.11. [Includes list of Lucas-Scuddamore family deeds relating to Axbridge, Loxton, Stogursey, etc.]

Dorset and Somerset deeds held at Warwick Record Office and Birmingham Reference Library are listed in:

FRY, C. R. 'Records outside the two counties', G.T., 2(4), 1977, p.52, 3(1), 1978, p.8-9 & 13, & 3(2), 1978, p.29.

There are also a number of lists of court rolls and other documents:

FRY, E. A. 'Somerset court rolls', N.Q.S.D., 4, 1894-5, p.243-5. [Calendar of court rolls, ministers accounts, rentals, etc., held at Lambeth Palace Library]

FRY, E. A. 'Surveys of manors in Somerset and Dorset', N.Q.S.D., 10, 1907, p.64-5. [List of surveys amongst the Miscellaneous books of the Land Revenue Dept. in the Public Record Office]

N[ATHAN], M. 'Documents relating to Somerset in the custody of the Ecclesiastical Commissioners', N.Q.S.D., 21, 1935, p.37-8. [List of court rolls at the Public Record Office]

NATHAN, Matthew. 'Documents relating to Somerset in the custody of Winchester College', N.Q.S.D., 21, 1935, p.56-60. [Relating especially to Long Load, Milborne Port, and Seavington]

The process of enclosing land from open field gave rise to many documents; enclosure awards usually include complete lists of landowners and tenants, and are consequently invaluable for genealogists. The awards for Somerset are listed in:

TATE, W. E. Somerset enclosure acts and awards; also, a detailed list of the enclosure award maps. Frome: Butler & Tanner for S.A.N.H.S., 1948.

Credit in pre-industrial England was often extended on bond. Bonds registered at Salisbury by merchants of Dorset and Somerset are listed in:

'Statute merchant bonds', N.Q.S.D., 10, 1907, p.327-30; 11, 1909, p.9-12, 159-63, 256-60, 357-9; 12, 1911, p.14-16, 66-8, 155-7 & 205-8.

In the late 18th and 19th centuries, the modern insurance business began. Insurance policies can be of great value to genealogists, as is demonstrated by:

HAWKINGS, David. 'Sun Insurance policies: country departments', G.T., 2(1), 1976, p.7. [Gives examples of John Wilcox of Taunton, 1825, & Robert Jarratt of Wellington, 1824]

B. PRIVATE ESTATES

Many families have preserved deeds and papers relating to their estates. A number of these have been printed. One of the largest estates in the West Country was surveyed in 1525:

STOATE, T. L. A survey of West Country manors, 1525: the lands of Cecily, Marchioness of Dorset, Lady Harington & Bonville, in Cornwall, Devon, Dorset, Somerset, Wiltshire. Almondsbury: the editor, 1979.

Other family estate papers which have been published include:

LYTE, H. C. Maxwell, ed. Two registers formerly belonging to the family of Beauchamp of Hatch. Somerset Record Society, 35. [ ]: the Society, 1920. [14th c. compilation, mainly concerned with Stoke-sub-Hamdon, Donden, Welton, Somerton, & Widcombe, in the 13th c.]

DACOMBE, J. M. J. 'Deeds with reference to the Dacombe family', N.Q.S.D., 20, 1930-32, p.34-5.

DUNNING, Robert W., ed. The Hylle cartulary. Somerset record Society, 69. Taunton: the Society, 1968. [15th c. Includes an account of the Fichet family]

JONES, W. 'Manuscript book of the fifteenth century lately found in the Bishops' registry at Exeter', Notes & gleanings ... Devon & Cornwall, 2, 1889, p.161-2. [Deeds of Montacutes, Earls of Salisbury, Beauchamp, & Neville, in Somerset, Devon, Dorset, etc.]

VANES, Jean, ed. The ledger of John Smythe, 1538-1550. Bristol Record Society, 28. London: H.M.S.O., 1974.

'Richard Strode's rental', N.Q.S.D., 12, 1911, p.35-7. [1447-8]

Many estate records relating to particular localities are available in printed form, and are listed here by place:

ALFOXTON

BATTEN, John. 'Alfoxton, Wordeston, Burton and Tokeswell: copies of old deeds ...', N.Q.S.D., 7, 1901, p.149-50. [Medieval]

ALHAMPTON

BATTEN, John. 'Alhampton, Churchill and Pokerleston (Puxton)', N.Q.S.D., 7, 1901, p.69-72, & 7, 1901, p.103-6. [Deeds showing descent through Fitzpayn, Kelly, Coryton; also will of Thomas Kelly, 1509]

ALLERTON

COLEMAN, Prebendary. 'The descent of the manor of Allerton', S.A.N.H.S., 45(2), 1899, p.25-50. [Medieval]

COLEMAN, Prebendary. 'The manor of Allerton and its tenants, 1530-1866', S.A.N.H.S., 46(2), 1900, p.65-108. [Includes pedigree of Bower, 15-17th c., manorial survey, 1650, & biographical notes on rectors, 15-19th c.]

BANWELL

'Banwell court rolls, 1714-1721', N.Q.S.D., 16, 1920, p.289-94.

BATH

KEMP, B. R., & SHORROCKS, D. M. M., eds. Medieval deeds of Bath and district. Somerset Record Society, 73. Castle Cary: the Society, 1974. [Includes genealogies of Forde, Malreward, & Husee]

SCHICKLE, C. W., ed. Ancient deeds belonging to the Corporation of Bath, XIII-XVI cent. Bath: Bath Records Society, 1921.

BISHOPS LYDEARD

GRESWELL, William. 'Chapel of St. Mary in Bishops' Lydeard', N.Q.S.D., 7, 1901, p.266-7. [Survey, 1652]

BROADWAY

S., J. W. 'Broadway, Somerset', N.Q.S.D., 7, 1901, p.268. [List of tenants, 1555]

BRUTON

'The Bruton audit, 1666', N.Q.S.D., 12, 1911, p.119-28. See also p.175-6. [Probably a list of rents due to the Crown; includes many local names]

'Bruton deeds at Coker Court', N.Q.S.D., 5, 1897-8, p.235-8. [14-15th c.]

WEAVER, F. W. 'Foundation deed of Bruton School', N.Q.S.D., 3, 1893, p.241-8. [Deed of 1519]

BURTON

See Alfoxton

CASTLE CARY

G., A. W. 'Castle Cary court roll, 1649-50', N.Q.S.D., 5, 1897-8, p.315-7. [Transcript]

W[EAVER], F. W. 'Manor of Castle Cary', N.Q.S.D., 15, 1917, p.88-91. [Extract from court roll, 1687]

CARHAMPTON

See Dunster

CATASH

See Stone

CHARD

WOODWARD, G. H. 'The purchase of Chard chantry lands in 1548', N.Q.S.D., 31,1980-5, p.201-5. [Includes list of tenants]

CHEDDAR

COLEMAN, Preb. The descent of the manor of Cheddar-Hannam. Wells: D. Woodhams, 1904.

CHURCHILL

See Alfoxton

CLEVEDON

'The descent of the manor of Clevedon', S.A.N.H.S., 27(1), 1881, p.17-28.

COMBE FLOREY

BATCHELOR, V. A. 'The manor of Combe Florey', S.A.N.H.S., 83(2), 1937, p.113-25. [Descent of the manor, 12-19th c.]

CRANDON CUM PURITON

MONDAY, A. J. 'Court rolls of the manor of Crandon cum Puriton', N.Q.S.D., 6, 1899, p.250-4. [Extracts listing tenants, etc., 17th c.]

CROWCOMBE

'Craucombe deeds', N.Q.S.D., 6, 1899, p.159-62 & 204-7. [Abstracts of 28 deeds]

CUCKLINGTON

'Lands in Cucklington and Wincanton', N.Q.S.D., 13, 1913, p.316-7.

CURRY RIVEL

CHANTER, J. F. 'The court rolls of the manor of Curry Rivel in the years of the Black Death, 1348-9', S.A.N.H.S., 56(2), 1910, p.85-135. [Includes list of tenants, 1347, & extracts from 1348-9 court roll]

DUNSTER

KILLE, H. W. 'West Somerset deeds', N.Q.S.D., 18, 1926, p.155-6. [Five 16-17th c. deeds concerning Dunster & Carhampton]

LYTE, H. C. Maxwell, ed. Documents and extracts illustrating the history of the honour of Dunster. Somerset Record Society, 33. Taunton: the Society, 1917-18.

LYTE, Sir H. C. Maxwell. Historical notes on some Somerset manors formerly connected with the honour of Dunster. Extra series. Taunton: Somerset Record Society, 1931.

EAST WOODLANDS

DANIEL, W. E. 'Manors of East Woodlands and Frome Vallis, Somerset', N.Q.S.D., 5, 1897-8, p.249-51. [17th c. legal opinion regarding conveyances of the manor from Leversedge to Vavasor and Thynne]

EVERCREECH

W[EAVER], F. W. 'Evercreech manor roll', N.Q.S.D., 11, 1909, p.227-46.

'Somerset archives at Lambeth Palace Library', N.Q.S.D., 8, 1903, p.169-72, & 209-12. [Court rolls for Evercreech, 1379 & 1414]

FROME

'Frome charity deeds', N.Q.S.D., 2, 1891, p.161-2 & 267-70. [12-13th c. deeds]

FROME SELWOOD

THOMPSON, E. Margaret. 'Charters relating to Frome-Selwood', N.Q.S.D., 7, 1901, p.246-9 & 305-9. [Medieval]

HORSINGTON

DANIEL, W. E. 'Land charters in Horsington, Somerset', N.Q.S.D., 14, 1915, p.70-74. [Medieval]

'Horsington court roll (Somerset)', N.Q.S.D., 5, 1897-8, p.353-4. [Transcript of 14th or 15th c. roll]

ILCHESTER

COX, G. Stevens, ed. An Ilchester (Somerset) rent roll of the XVI century hitherto unpublished. Ilchester & District occasional papers, 3. St. Peter Port: Toucan Press, 1972.

KINGSDON

VIVIAN-NEAL, A. W. 'Illustrations of the manorial system drawn from the history of Kingsdon', S.A.N.H.S., 103, 1958/9, p.22-70. See also 104, 1959/60, p141-3. [Descent of the manor, including pedigree of Gouvis, 12-14th c.]

LIMINGTON

BATTEN, John. 'The early owners of Limington', S.A.N.H.S., 33(2), 1887, p.137-45.

MILVERTON

'Manor of Preston Bowyer in Milverton parish, Somerset', N.Q.S.D., 6, 1899, p.327-36. [Survey, 1650]

NETTLECOMBE

T., W. C. 'Charters relating to Nettlecombe, Co. Somerset, and the families of Mareschall, [Earls of Pembroke] and of Ralegh, transcribed from originals in the posseession of Sir John Trevelyan, Bart', Collectanea genealogica et topographica, 2, 1835, p.163-6. [Latin transcript, medieval]

NORTH CADBURY

SHERWOOD, G. F. T. 'Deeds relating to North and South Cadbury', N.Q.S.D., 3, 1893, p.109-10 & 335-6; 4, 1895, p.164-6. [Deeds concerning Huchings, Medlycott, Newman & Bennett families, 17-19th c.]

NORTH PERROT

BATTEN, John. 'Notes on North Perrot', S.A.N.H.S., 41(2), 1895, p.73-91. [Includes abstracts of 23 medieval deeds]

ORCHARDLEIGH

McGARVIE, Michael. 'The Orchardleigh charters', N.Q.S.D., 31, 1980-85, p.185-9. [Transcript of 5 Orchardleigh charters]

POYNTINGTON

LYTE, Sir H. C. Maxwell. 'The manor of Poyntington', S.A.N.H.S., 82(2), 1936, p.203-216. [Descent of the manor]

PUXTON

See Alfoxton

SANDFORD ORCAS

FRY, Edw. Alex. , & THORP, J. Disney. 'Descent of the manor of Sandford Orcas', S.A.N.H.S., 69(2), 1923, p.38-48.

SOUTH CADBURY

See North Cadbury

STAPLE FITZPAINE

RADFORD, W. Locke. 'Staple Fitzpaine court roll, 1531', N.Q.S.D., 18, 1926, p.187-9. [Transcript]

STOKE SUB HAMDON

BATTEN, John. 'Stoke under Hamdon, in connection with Sir Matthew de Gournay, Kt., and the Duchy of Cornwall', S.A.N.H.S., 40, 1894, p.236-71. [Includes manorial presentment, 1616, giving names of tenants, and a pedigree of Gournay, 13-15th c.]

STONE

BATTEN, John. 'Hundreds of Stone and Catash, Somerset', N.Q.S.D., 7, 1901, p.120-6 & 159-64. [17th c. court roll]

TAUNTON

HOOK, Arthur J. 'Catalogue of the documents in the Exchequer at Taunton Castle', S.A.N.H.S., 70(2), 1924, p.97-103. [Records of the manor of Taunton Dene]

MONDAY, A. J. 'The manor of Taunton Deane: names of the tenants in the year 1450', Western antiquary, 4, 1885, p.216.

SHEPPARD, H. B. Courts leet and the court leet of the borough of Taunton. Taunton: Barnicott & Pearce, 1909.

'Priorswood Farm books', G.T., 8(2), p.50. [Names from account book of a Taunton farmer, 1825-40]

TOKESWELL

See Alfoxton

UP MUDFORD

'Up Mudford', N.Q.S.D., 23, 1942, p.221-6, 237-9, & 261-4. [Abstracts of 37 deeds, 1554-1655]

WALCOT

HAMMOND, J. J. 'Walcot tenants roll, 1693', N.Q.S.D., 18, 1926, p.150-3.

WELLOW

'Wellow parish, Somerset', N.Q.S.D., 12, 1911, p.227-9. [Includes abstracts of 11 17th c. deeds]

WELLS

SHILTON, Dorothy, & HOLWORTHY, Richard, ed. Wells city charters. Somerset Record Society, 46. Taunton: the Society, 1932.

WINCANTON

'Wincanton deeds', N.Q.S.D., 13, 1913, p.315-6. [15th c.]

See also Cucklington

WIVELISCOMBE

'Wiveliscombe court roll', N.Q.S.D., 21, 1935, p.223-7. [16th c.]

WORDESTON

See Alfoxton

C. ECCLESIASTICAL ESTATES AND CARTULARIES, ETC.

In the medieval period, a great deal of property was owned by ecclesiastical institutions such as monasteries, chantries, dioceses, etc. Ecclesiastical estate records have survived much better than those of private families, especially where they fell into the hands of the government, and many are in print. Many estate records of the county's nunneries, together with lists of clergy, etc., are printed in:

HUGO, Thomas. The medieval nunneries of the county of Somerset and diocese of Bath and Wells. London: J. R. Smith, 1867.

A general survey of chantry lands just before the dissolution is provided by:

GREEN, Emanuel, ed. The survey and rental of the chantries, colleges and free chapels, guilds, fraternities, lamps and obits in the county of Somerset as returned in the 2nd year of King Edward VI, A.D. 1548. Somerset Record Society, 2. Taunton: the Society, 1888.

This may be complemented by:

WOODWARD, G. H., ed. Calendar of Somerset chantry grants, 1548-1603. Somerset Record Society, 77. Taunton: the Society, 1982.

Printed records of particular ecclesiastical bodies include:

BARLINCH

WEAVER, F. W. 'Barlinch Priory', S.A.N.H.S., 54(2), 1908, p.79-106. [Includes list of priors and benefactors, deed extracts, pedigrees of Say, 13th c., Besilles, 13-16th c., Inquisition post mortem of Thomas Besilles, 1458; will of Piers de Besyles, 1424, etc]

BATH

HUNT, William, ed. Two chartularies of the priory of St. Peter at Bath. 1. The chartulary in ms. no. cxi in the library of Corpus Christi College, Cambridge. II: Calendar of the ms. register in the library of the Hon. Society of Lincoln's Inn. Somerset Record Society, 7. [ ]: the Society, 1893.

BRISTOL. ST. AUGUSTINE'S

BEACHCROFT, Gwen, & SABIN, Arthur, eds. Two compotus rolls of Saint Augustine's Abbey, Bristol, for 1491-2 and 1511-12. Bristol record Society, 9. Bristol: the Society, 1938. [Includes property in Somerset]

BRISTOL. ST. MARKS

ROSS, C. D., ed. Cartulary of St. Marks, Bristol. Bristol Record Society, 21. Bristol: the Society, 1959. [Includes property at Pawlett, Weare,etc.]

BRUTON

Two cartularies of the Augustinian Priory of Bruton and the Cluniac Priory of Montacute in the county of Somerset. Somerset Record Society, 8. Taunton: the Society, 1894.

GULLEY, J. L. M. 'The Bruton chartulary', British Museum quarterly, 27, 1963, p.190-202.

TREMLETT, T. D. Calendar of the manuscripts belonging to the King's School, Bruton, 1297-1826. Bruton: [the School?], 1939. [Includes deeds, registers, etc., also names of governors and attorneys, etc.]

BUCKLAND

WEAVER, F. W., ed. A cartulary of Buckland priory in the county of Somerset. Somerset Record Society, 25. Taunton: the Society, 1909.

CLEEVE

HUGO, Thomas. 'On the charters and other archives of Cleeve Abbey', S.A.N.H.S., 6(2), 1855, p.17-73.

WEAVER, F. W. 'Cleeve Abbey', S.A.N.H.S., 52(2), 1906, p.1-41. [Includes extracts from deeds, lists of abbots & benefactors, etc.]

GLASTONBURY

JACKSON, John Edward, ed. Liber Henrici de Soliaco Abbatis Glaston: an inquisition of the manor of Glastonbury Abbey, of the year M.C.LXXXIV ... Roxburghe Club. London: J. B. Nichols & Son, 1882.

NEVIL, Edmund R. 'Glastonbury Abbey accounts', N.Q.S.D., 12, 1911, p.146-50. [Transcripts of various brief account rolls, 1537-9]

WATKIN, Aelred, ed. The great chartulary of Glastonbury. Somerset Record Society, 59, 63, & 64. Taunton: the Society, 1947-1956. [Numerous pedigrees are found in vol.63]

Rentalia et custumaria Michaelis de Ambresbury, 1235-1252, et Rogeri de Ford, 1252-1261, abbatum monasterii beatae Mariae Glastoniae, with an excursus on manorial land tenures, by C. J. Elton, and introductory historical notes by Edmund Hobhouse and T. S. Holmes. Somerset Record Society, 5. [ ]: the Society, 1891.

WEAVER, F. W., ed. A feodary of Glastonbury Abbey, 1342. Somerset Record Society, 26. Taunton: the Society, 1910.

FLOWER, R. 'Last pre-dissolution survey of Glastonbury Abbey lands', British Museum quarterly, 10(2), p.69-72. [General discussion of mss.]

'Index to Abbot Monington's Secretum', N.Q.S.D., 12, 1911, p.273-80, 321-8, & 356-63; 13, 1913, p.41-8, 89-96, & 136-44. [List of Glastonbury charters]

KEYNSHAM

WEAVER, F. W. 'Keynsham Abbey', S.A.N.H.S., 53(2), 1907, p.15-63. [Includes list of abbots, deed extracts, etc.]

MONTACUTE

See Bruton

MUCHELNEY

BATES, E. H., ed. Two cartularies of the Benedictine abbeys of Muchelney and Athelney in the county of Somerset. Somerset Record Society, 14. Taunton: the Society, 1899.

STEEP HOLME

HARBIN, E. H. Bates. 'The Priory of St. Michael on the Steep Holme', S.A.N.H.S., 62(2), 1916, p.26-45. [Includes deed abstracts]

STOGURSEY

TREMLETT, T. D., & BLAKISTON, Noel, ed. Stogursey charters: charters and other documents relating to the property of the alien priory of Stogursey, Somerset, now belonging to Eton College. Somerset Record Society, 61. Taunton: the Society, 1949. [Includes pedigrees of Curci, Columbers, Regni, & Fitzurse]

GRESWELL, W. H. P. 'The alien Priory of Stoke Courcy', S.A.N.H.S., 43(2), 1897, p.62-83. [Stogursey; includes deed extracts from chartulary]

TEMPLECOMBE

'Calendar of all the charters and muniments of Templecombe and of all other the manors to the same belonging in divers counties renewed by William Hulles, brother of the Hospital of St. John of Jerusalem in England, and Preceptor in the 20th year of the reign of King Richard the Second ...', N.Q.S.D. , 21, 1935, p.86-92.

HARVEY, John H. 'Templar holdings in East Somerset', N.Q.S.D., 31, 1980-85, p.135-41. [Includes rental, 1505]

WELLS

BIRD, W. H. B., & PALEY, W., eds. Calendar of the manuscripts of the Dean and Chapter of Wells. 2 vols. Cd. 7106. London: H.M.S.O., 1907-14.

CHURCH, C. M. 'Gifts to the church of St. Andrew in Wells by land-owners in Somerset during the episcopate of Bishop Reginald Fitzjocelin, 1174-1191', Western antiquary, 6(1), 1886, p.1-5.

Wells Cathedral Commoners' accounts, 1327-1600. Wells: Friends of Wells Cathedral, 1984.

Wells Cathedral Escheators' accounts, 1369-1600. 2 vols. [Wells]: privately printed, 1988.

CHAPTER 15
NATIONAL, COUNTY, AND PAROCHIAL ADMINISTRATION

A. NATIONAL AND COUNTY

Most of Somerset's leading families have at one time or another sent a member to represent the county or a local borough in Parliament. Much information on these individuals is contained in:

BATES-HARBIN, S. W. Members of Parliament for the county of Somerset. Taunton: Somerset Archaeological and Natural History Society, 1932-9. [Originally issued as supplements to S.A.N.H.S., 78-85, 1932-9.]

BATES-HARBIN, S. W. 'Somerset members of Parliament', Somerset year book, 36, 1937, p.37-9.

The most important official in county government, from the Norman conquest onwards, was the sheriff. Sheriffs are listed in:

RAWLINS, S. W. The sheriffs of Somerset from the eleventh to the twentieth centuries. Taunton: Hammett & Co., for S.A.N.H.S., 1968. [Reprinted from S.A.N.H.S., 106-11, 1962-7, passim]

From the 15th century onwards, the role of local justices became of ever increasing importance. A number of works identify them:

W., F. W. 'Commissions of the Peace, 1413-1414', N.Q.S.D., 12, 1911, p.163-4. [List of justices for Somerset and Dorset]

'Somerset justices, 1584', N.Q.S.D., 2, 1891, p.59-60.

MONDAY, A. J. 'Somerset J.P's in 1685', N.Q.S.D., 10, 1907, p.308.

National and county administration has produced a wide range of records of value to the genealogist, some of which have been published. They are listed here in chronological order:

CHADWYCK-HEALEY, Charles E. H., ed. Somersetshire pleas, civil and criminal, from the rolls of the itinerant justices, close of 12th century-41 Henry III. Somerset Record Society, 11. Taunton: the Society, 1897. [Later pleas have been edited by Lionel Landon, Somerset Record Society, nos.36, 41, & 44, 1923-1929]

'Forest pleas, Somerset. Selwood', N.Q.S.D., 5, 1897-8, p.270-3. [List of tenants; 13th c.]

STEVENS, Douglas. 'A Somerset coroner's roll, 1315-1321', N.Q.S.D., 31, 1980-85.

DILKS, T. Bruce. 'Bridgwater and the insurrection of 1381', S.A.N.H.S., 73, 1927, p.57-69. [Includes list of rebels]

LYTE, H. C. Maxwell. 'Knights and squires in Somerset and Dorset', N.Q.S.D., 16, 1920, p.162-3. [List of potential jurors, 1406]

BRADFORD, Gladys, ed. Proceedings in the court of star chamber in the reigns of Henry VII and Henry VIII. Somerset Record Society, 27. Taunton: the Society, 1911. [Transcripts of all Somerset cases]

BATES, E. H., ed. Quarter sessions records for the county of Somerset. Somerset Record Society, 23-4, 28, & 34. Taunton: the Society, 1907-1919. [Vol. 1. 1607-1625. Vol. 2. 1625-1639. Vol. 3. 1646-1660. Includes a pedigree showing the connection of Fitz-Payne, Walton, Venables, Hinkley, Mareschall, Swynnerton, Whitmore, & Alsager. Vol. 4. 1666-1677, edited by M.C.B. Dawes.]

BARNES, Thomas G., ed. Somerset assize orders, 1629-1640. Somerset Record Society, 66. Taunton: the Society, 1959

COCKBURN, J. S., ed. Somerset assize orders, 1640-1659. Somerset Record Society, 72. Taunton: the Society, 1971. [Includes a list of Somerset attorneys, 1649-60]

COCKBURN, J. S., ed. Western circuit assize orders, 1629-1648: a calendar. Camden 4th series, 17. London: Royal Historical Society, 1976.

DUNNING, Robert. The Monmouth rebellion: a complete guide to the rebellion and bloody assizes. Wimborne: Dovecote Press, 1984.

WIGFIELD, W. M. The Monmouth rebels, 1685. Somerset Record Society, 79. Taunton: The Society, 1985. [Includes a full roll-call of the rebels, including places of origin - which were mainly in Somerset, Dorset, and Devon]

SYMONDS, Henry. 'Somerset registered estates in 1717', N.Q.S.D., 6, 1899, p.208-9. [Estates confiscated after the Jacobite rebellion of 1715]

The reports of the Commissioners ... to enquire concerning charities in England and Wales, relating to the county of Somerset, 1819-1837. 2 vols. London: P. S. King, 1890. [Reprinted from the Parliamentary papers; includes many notes on deeds, wills, etc.]

B. PAROCHIAL ADMINISTRATION

The records of parochial government - the accounts of churchwardens, overseers, and other parish officers, settlement papers, rate lists, etc - contain a good deal of information for the genealogist. They frequently provide the names, if nothing else, of the humble mass of the poor, who otherwise went unrecorded. Surviving Somerset records are listed in two works:

KING, John Edward, ed. Inventory of parochial documents in the diocese of Bath and Wells and the county of Somerset. Taunton: Somerset County Council, 1938.

A handlist of the records of the Boards of Guardians in the county of Somerset preserved in the Somerset Record Office. Taunton: Harold King, 1949.

See also:

MUNCKTON, Thelma. 'Bastardy & settlement: papers at the Somerset County Record Office', G.T., 9(1), 1983, p.22-3.

Somerset parochial records have been the subject of many books and articles. Some of those likely to be of genealogical interest are listed here:

AXBRIDGE

HUNT, William. 'On the charters and municipal government of Axbridge', S.A.N.H.S., 15(2), 1868-9, p.6-20.

BATH

FERRIS, J. P. 'Bath: the Corporation in 1680', N.Q.S.D. , 30, 1974-9, p.275-8. [List of aldermen and common councilmen]

KING, Austin J., & WATTS, B. H. The municipal records of Bath, 1189 to 1604. London: Elliot Stock; Bath: J. Davies, [1885].

WARDLE, F. D., ed. The accounts of the chamberlains of the city of Bath, 1568-1602. Somerset Record Society, 38. Taunton: the Society, 1923.

BATH. St. Michael's

PEARSON, C. B., ed. The churchwardens accounts of the church & parish of S. Michael without the North Gate, Bath, 1349-1575. Taunton: Cheston & Cheasley for S.A.N.H.S., 1878. Supplement to S.A.N.H.S., 23-6, 1877-80.

See also under Croscombe

BISHOP'S HULL

TITE, Charles. 'Bishop's Hull, Somerset, new chancel, 1523', N.Q.S.D., 7, 1901, p.264-6. [Deposition, including names and ages of many parishioners]

BRIDGWATER

ODGERS, J. Edwin. 'A short report on some ms accounts of the commonalty of Bridgwater', S.A.N.H.S., 23(), 1877, p.38-48. [Receivers and bailiffs' rolls, 14-15th c.]

DILKS, Thomas Bruce, et al, eds. Bridgwater borough archives. Somerset Record Society, 48, 53, 58, 60, & 70. [ ]: the Society, 1933-1971. [Pt. 1. 1200-1377. Pt. 2. 1377-1399. Pt. 3. 1400-1445. Pt. 4. 1445-1468. Pt. 5. 1468-1485.]

RILEY, Henry Thomas. 'The county records of Somerset', in Third report of the Royal Commission on Historical Manuscripts. London: H.M.S.O., 1872. [Includes description of Bridgwater & Wells archives]

SLOCOMBE, I. M. 'The Bridgwater Court of Record in the 18th century', S.A.N.H.S., 111, 1967, p.38-50.

CASTLE CARY

GRAFTON, A. W. 'Castle Cary churchwardens' accounts, 1628 to 1699', S.A.N.H.S., 36(2), 1890, p.60-69. [Includes extracts]

CHURCHILL

'Licence to beg granted to an ejected Irish minister in 1643', N.Q.S.D., 2, 1891, p.11-12. [Entries of doles in Churchill churchwardens' accounts explained by reference to a licence to beg granted to James Cleland]

COMBE ST. NICHOLAS

JONES, I. Fitzroy. 'Combe St. Nicholas churchwardens' presentments', N.Q.S.D., 23, 1942, p.83-5. [Late 17th c.]

CROSCOMBE

HOBHOUSE, Edmund, ed. Church-wardens' accounts of Croscombe, Pilton, Yatton, Tintinhull, Morebath, and St. Michael's, Bath, ranging from A.D. 1349 to 1560. Somerset Record Society, 4. Taunton: the Society, 1890.

CROWCOMBE

'Crowcombe tythes, 1686', G.T., 9(1), 1983, p.25.

DUNSTER

HANCOCK, F. Dunster church and priory: their history and architectural features. Taunton: Barnicott & Pearce, 1905. [Includes monumental inscriptions, notes on parish registers, extracts from accounts, lists of churchwardens and overseers, etc.]

FIDDINGTON

DODDERIDGE, Sidney E. 'Fiddington churchwarden's accounts', N.Q.S.D., 19, 1929, p.42-3. [Includes roster of parishioners due to serve as churchwardens, 17th c.]

FROME

CROCKER, A. A brief historical account of the almshouse and school charities within the parish of Frome ... Frome: Crocker & Sons, 1815. [Includes extracts from wills, names of trustees, etc.]

GLASTONBURY

DANIEL, W. E. 'Churchwardens' accounts, St. John's, Glastonbury', N.Q.S.D., 4, 1894-5, p.89-96, 137-44, 185-92, 235-40, 250-3, 281-8, 329-36, & 379-84; 5, 1897-8, p.45-8 & 93-6. [14-16th c.]

DANIEL, Prebendary. 'The accounts of St. John's church, Glastonbury', S.A.N.H.S., 48(2), 1902, p.11-21. [Includes list of churchwardens, 14-17th c., & chaplains, 14-15th c.]

'Valuation of the repairs of Glastonbury almshouses, 30 May 1722', N.Q.S.D., 17, 1923, p.138-9. [Includes names of many parochial officers and inhabitants]

ILCHESTER

COX, J. Stevens, ed. Ilchester borough records of the 17th century. Ilchester & district occasional papers, 10. St. Peter Port: Toucan Press, 1978.

KINGSDON

HENNING, G. S. 'Churchwardens accounts of Kingsdon, Somerset', N.Q.S.D., 6, 1899, p.32-41. [Includes extracts, with list of churchwardens, 1587-1688, & church rate, 1656]

KINGSTON ST. MARY

RAMSEY, R. W. 'Kingston St. Mary overseers' accounts', N.Q.S.D., 23, 1942, p.339-45. [17th c.]

RAMSAY, Robert W. 'Parish records of Kingston St. Mary, 1641-1852', S.A.N.H.S., 87, 1941, p.85-105. [General discussion, with few names]

LANGPORT

ROSS, D. Melvile. 'The papers of the former Corporation of Langport, 1596-1888', S.A.N.H.S., 53(2), 1907, p.148-73. [Includes a list of documents]

LYDEARD ST. LAWRENCE

BATES, E. H. 'Lydeard S. Lawrence: churchwardens' accounts, 1524-1559', N.Q.S.D., 7, 1901, p.212-9.

MOREBATH

See Croscombe

NYNEHEAD

PRIDEAUX, W. de C. 'An early portion of the churchwardens' accounts of All Saints, Nynehead (1668-1684)', S.A.N.H.S., 58(2), 1912, p.60-104. [Transcript]

PILTON

HOLMES, T.S. 'Churchwardens' accounts in the parish of Pilton', N.Q.S.D., 1, 1890, p.12-13.

See also Croscombe

SHEPTON MALLET

HEARD, Herbert. Shepton Mallet notes on the charities of the town. Shepton Mallet: A Byrt & Son, 1903. [Includes extracts from deeds & wills, lists of trustees, etc.]

SOMERTON

HAYWARD, Douglas L. 'Notes on Somerton churchwardens' accounts, 1641-1747', S.A.N.H.S., 39(2), 1893, p.67-86. [Includes list of ratepayers, 1641, & churchwardens, 1641-1740, etc.]

SWAINSWICK

PEACH, R. E. M. The annals of the parish of Swainswick (near the City of Bath), with abstracts of the parish registers,, the church accounts, and othe overseers books. London: Sampson Low, Marston, Searle & Rivington; Bath: Charles Hallett, 1890. [Includes extracts from the register, 1537-1800, pedigrees of Gunning, Whittington & Hyde-Clark, list of churchwardens and incumbents, monumental inscriptions, extracts from accounts, etc.]

TAUNTON

TITE, C. 'Mayors of Taunton', N.Q.S.D., 12, 1911, p.259-61. [List, 1627-1877]

SHEPPARD, H. Byard. 'Courts leet and the court leet of the borough of Taunton', S.A.N.H.S., 55(2), 1909, p.1-65. [Includes list of constables, 15-20th c.]

WHITTY, R. G. H. The court of Taunton in the 16th and 17th centuries: a study in the legal and social history of Taunton under the Tudors and Stuarts. Taunton: Goodman, 1934.

TINTINHULL

See Croscombe

TRULL

JONES, I. Fitzroy. 'Aspects of poor law administration, seventeenth to nineteenth centuries, from Trull overseers' accounts', S.A.N.H.S., 95, 1950, p.74-105. [General discussion, with few names]

WEDMORE

ROSE, Cuthbert Arthur. Wedmore's moors and the enclosure acts of the 18th century, together with some records of the parish relating to this subject and period. Wedmore: the author, 1982. [Includes enclosure award, 1778, rate books of 1791 & 1840, monumental inscriptions, extracts from Kelly's 1883 directory, etc]

WELLS

See Bridgwater

WESTON ZOYLAND

STURDY, Philip. 'Westonzoyland church records', N.Q.S.D., 19, 1929, p.253-8. [Extracts from the parish register and churchwardens' accounts relating to the Battle of Sedgemoor, 1685]

WINSFORD

DICKER, W. 'Winsford parish documents', N.Q.S.D., 3, 1893, p.334-5. [Apprenticeship indenture for George Webber, 1660, & settlement certificate for Mary Pearse, 1692]

WRINGTON

SCARTH, Preb. 'Ancient churchwardens' accounts, Wrington', Proceedings of the Bath Natural History & Antiquarian Field Club, 6, 1873, p.444-54.

YATTON

EDWARDS, A. C. 'The medieval churchwardens' accounts of St. Mary's Church, Yatton', N.Q.S.D., 32, 1986- , p.536-47.

HARRISON, John. 'The spire of Yatton church', N.Q.S.D., 7, 1901, p.335-8. [Extracts from churchwardens's accounts, 16th c., giving many names]

See also Croscombe

YEOVIL

GOODCHILD, John. 'Elizabethan Yeovil, as recorded in churchwardens' accounts', S.A.N.H.S., 88, 1942, p.56-72.

N., J. G. 'Account of the proctors of the church of Yeovil, Co. Somerset, 36 Hen. VI, 1457-8', Collectanea topographica et genealogica, 3, 1836, p.134-41.

CHAPTER 16
EDUCATION

The records of schools can provide the genealogist with a great deal of information. For the history of Somerset schools in the medieval period, see:

ORME, Nicholas. Education in the West of England, 1066-1548: Cornwall, Devon, Dorset, Gloucestershire, Somerset, Wiltshire. Exeter: University of Exeter, 1976.

There are many histories of individual schools, and a few school registers have been published; the latter are particularly helpful. School histories usually list head teachers; they may also include the names of assistant teachers and/or pupils. Some, of course, are of much more value to the genealogist than others. The following list is not comprehensive; rather it identifies some of those school histories which have genealogical value.

BATH

BLAND, C., et al. Bath College register (1878-1909). Worthing: [ ], 1948. See also addenda & corrigenda, 1949.

BRUTON

FOX, A. D. Kings School, Bruton, register. 3rd ed. London: Oxford University Press, 1911.

TREMLETT, T. D. 'Some additions to the register of King's School, Bruton', N.Q.S.D., 25, 1950, p.217. [List of 30 pupils, 1769-92]

TREMLETT, T. D. 'The governors of Bruton School during the sixteenth century', N.Q.S.D., 22, 1938, p.59-62.

WEAVER, F. W. 'Head masters of Bruton School', N.Q.S.D., 5, 1897-8, p.102-7. See also 22, 1938, p.221-2. [List, 1539-1890, with brief biographical notes]

HOBHOUSE, Henry. A short history of Hugh Sexeys Hospital, Bruton, and its endowments. Taunton: Barnicott & Pearce, 1925. [Includes list of visitors, 1638-1922, & masters, 1638-1901]

'Sexey's Hospital, Bruton, Somerset', N.Q.S.D., 14, 1915, p.151-3. [List of visitors]

Sexeys School, Bruton, Somerset: directory, 1891-1920. [Bruton: the School], 1921.

CREWKERNE

BARTELOT, R. Grosvenor. History of Crewkerne School, A.D. 1499-1899. Crewkerne: James Wheatley, 1899. [Includes register of 'foundationers', 1828-99, list of feoffees, 1558-1870, governors, 1876, etc]

DOWNSIDE

BIRT, Henry Norbert. Downside: the history of St. Gregory's School from the comencement at Douay to the present time. London: Kegan Paul, Trench, Trubner & Co., 1902. [Bath; includes biographical notes on 'Gregorian worthies', with list of priors or headmasters]

ILMINSTER

BAKER, J. 'Humphrey Walrond and Ilminster Grammar School', N.Q.S.D., 1, 1890, p.197-8. [Includes abstracts of foundation deed, 3 Ed.VI, including names]

KINGSWOOD

HASTLING, A. H. L. Register of Kingswood School. 3rd. ed. Brentford: [ ], 1923.

LANGPORT

'Headmasters of Langport Grammar School', N.Q.S.D., 8, 1903, p.215-6.

MONKTON COMBE

LACE, A. F. A goodly heritage: a history of Monkton Combe School, 1868 to 1967. Bath: the School, 1968. [Includes list of senior prefects, etc]

SIDCOT

BLASCHKO, M. D., ed. Sidcot School: register of old scholars, 1808-1958. Winscombe, Somerset: the School, c.1958.

TAUNTON

CHANNON, H. J. [Queens College, Taunton, old boys' directory]. Taunton: [the School], 1932.

RECORD, S. P. Proud century: the first hundred years of Taunton School. Taunton: E. Goodman, 1946 [Includes many names]

WICKS, A. T. 'Masters of Taunton Grammar School', N.Q.S.D ., 27, 1961, p.195-7. [List with biographical notes, 16-19th c.]

'Taunton School list', N.Q.S.D., 21, 1935, p.65-6. See also p.141. [Pupils in 1714]

Many Somersetians attended the universities, and their registers should be consulted for biographical details of students. See the companion volume to the present work, English genealogy: an introductory bibliography. Three works of particular relevance to Somerset are:

'Alumni of Caius College, Cambridge', N.Q.S.D., 1, 1890, p.107-9. [From Somerset and Dorset; includes genealogical notes]

ROBINSON, C. J. 'Admissions to St. John's College, Cambridge, of natives of Dorset and Somerset, inter 1666-1715', N.Q.S.D., 3, 1893, p.271-2.

GARDINER, Robert Barlow, ed. The registers of Wadham College, from 1613 to [1871]. 2 vols. London: G. Bell & Sons, 1889-97. [Founded by Thomas Wadham of Merifield, Somerset, the College attracted many West Country students, especially from Somerset, Dorset, and Devon]

AUTHOR INDEX

PLACE-NAME INDEX

101

FAMILY NAME INDEX

Hooper 34
Hopton 29
Horner 26, 29, 59
Horsey 29
How 34
Huchings 85
Huddesfield 35
Hulls 59
Hungerford 32, 66
Husee 83
Huyshe 29
Hyde 61
Hyde-Clark 93
Hylle 82
Hywysch 57
Ireland 22
Ireson 66
Isham 29, 58
Jackson 35
Jacob 29
Jarratt 82
Jennings 30
Jenyns 67
Jessop 38
Jones 59
Kelly 83
Keynes 29
King 29, 60
Kirton 29
Knight 30, 60
Lane 30
Langley 60
Langton 30
Lavor 30
Lawrence 30
Legg 30
Leir 30
Lethbridge 30
Leversedge 84
Leversegge 60
Levett 66
Linley 30
Lisle 30
Lloyd 68
Loader 16
Lockett 30
Loders 30
Long 30, 60, 66
Lovel 30
Lucas 81
Luttrell 32
Lyons 31
Lyte 31
McAdam 31
Magot 59
Malet 31
Malreward 83
Mareschall 85, 90
Marisco 31
Marks 60
Marriott-Dodington 31
Martin 21, 31
Medlycott 85
Melford 22
Meriet 31
Merrick 31

Messeter 60
Michel 26
Michell 31
Middleton 67
Midelney 32
Milborne 32
Moeles 32
Mohun 32
Molyns 32
Montacute 82
Montagu 32
Morrish 66
Muchgros 32
Musgrave 32
Muttlebury 32
Nash 67
Nashe 32
Neville 82
Newman 85
Norris 32
North 60
Norton 67
Notcutt 32
Nutcombe 33
Oaten 33
Oldmixon 33
Orchard 33
Pabenham 25
Paco 57
Palmer 67
Pardee 33
Parker 33
Parsons 30
Paulet 33, 66
Paull 33
Pearse 93
Pendilton 68
Penne 67
Penny 33
Peppin 33
Perrett 33
Phelips 34
Phelps 34
Phillipps 34
Pitman 30
Pitt 67
Plumley 34
Pomeroy 60
Pontesbury 57
Popham 34
Portman 34, 60
Poulet 67
Powell 34
Powlett 34
Prowse 34
Pym 34, 60
Pyne 34
Ralegh 39, 85
Rawle 34
Rawlins 34
Raymond 35
Reginald 77
Regni 88
Rendall 35
Retter 35
Reynolds 35
Reyny 35

Rocke 35
Rodney 35
Rogers 27, 35,
Rose 60, 67
Rosewell 35
Rosse 35
Russ 35
Russell 34, 60
St. Clair 35
Sagittary 60
Samborne 36
Savaric 77
Say 86
Scuddamore 81
Scutte 60
Seaman 28, 36
Seward 36
Seymour 36
Sharpe 36
Sheate 36
Sheppard 36
Shumack 36
Shute 36
Siderfin 36
Skrine 36
Skutt 36
Smith 32, 36, 60
Smith-Wyndham 34
Smyth 37
Smythe 82
Smythies 37
Snigg 37
Sparkeford 57
Spearing 16
Speke 37, 67
Stawell 37, 67
Staynings 37, 61
Stephens 22
Stevens-Loader 16
Stoate 37
Stocker 38
Stone 37, 68
Stourton 37, 62
Strangways 37
Strechleigh 26
Strode 38, 61, 82
Strong 38
Stuckey 38
Sturge 22
Swayne 66
Swinnerton 38
Swynnerton 90
Sydenham 38, 67
Symcoke 38
Symonds 38
Tanner 61
Tassell 38
Thorner 28
Thornton 61
Thynne 84
Titford 38
Tratt 38
Treat 38
Trenchard 67
Trevelyan 39, 85
Trock 57
Trott 38